AI BASICS FOR MANAGERS

AI BASICS FOR MANAGERS

A COMPREHENSIVE GUIDE FOR MANAGERS TO IMPLEMENT, MEASURE, AND OPTIMIZE AI IN BUSINESS OPERATIONS WITHIN THE AI REVOLUTION

AI FUNDAMENTALS

ANDREW HINTON

B

Book Bound
STUDIOS

This book is dedicated to all the forward-thinking business leaders, managers, and decision-makers boldly embracing the future. To those who understand that the key to success lies in continuous learning and adaptation. To those ready to harness artificial intelligence's power to drive their business growth and success. This book is for you. May it serve as your guide in navigating the complex world of AI and inspire you to lead your organization into the future confidently.

AI is the new electricity. It has the potential to transform every industry and to create huge economic value.

— ANDREW NG

CONTENTS

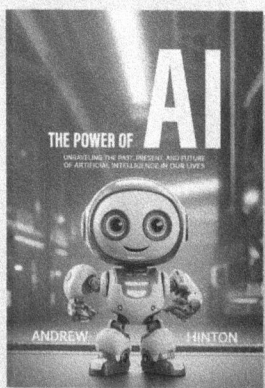

$10.99 ~~FREE EBOOK~~

Receive Your Free Copy of The Power of AI

SCAN ME

Or visit:
bookboundstudios.wixsite.com/andrew-hinton

INTRODUCTION TO AI FOR MANAGERS

The dawn of the 21st century has witnessed a technological revolution unlike any other in human history. At the forefront of this revolution is artificial intelligence (AI), a rapidly evolving field that has the potential to transform every aspect of our lives. As a manager in today's fast-paced business environment, it is crucial to understand the basics of AI and embrace its potential to drive innovation, efficiency, and growth within your organization.

The AI revolution is already well underway, with countless industries and sectors reaping the benefits of this groundbreaking technology. From healthcare and finance to manufacturing and retail, AI is reshaping the way we live, work, and interact with one another. As a manager, you are uniquely positioned to harness AI's power and lead your team into a future defined by data-driven decision-making, automation, and unparalleled efficiency.

However, embracing the AI revolution has its challenges. As with any disruptive technology, potential pitfalls and obstacles exist. This book aims to provide you with the knowledge and tools necessary to navigate the complex world of AI, ensuring you are well-equipped to make informed decisions and implement effective strategies within your organization.

In the following chapters, we will delve into the fundamentals of AI, exploring its history, key concepts, and various applications in the business world. We will also examine the ethical considerations and potential risks associated with AI and the steps you can take to mitigate these concerns. Finally, we will provide practical guidance on successfully integrating AI into your management practices, empowering you to lead your team into a future driven by artificial intelligence.

As you embark on this journey, remember that the AI revolution should not be feared or resisted. Rather, it is an opportunity to embrace change, foster innovation, and propel your organization to new heights. By understanding the basics of AI and adopting a multifaceted approach to its implementation, you can ensure that your team is well-prepared to thrive in a world increasingly defined by artificial intelligence. So, let us begin our exploration of AI for managers and unlock the potential of this transformative technology.

The Emergence of AI in the Business World

The dawn of the digital age has brought about a paradigm shift in the way businesses operate, and at the forefront of this revolution is Artificial Intelligence (AI). The concept of AI, which was once confined to science fiction, has now become an integral part of our daily lives. From virtual assistants like Siri and Alexa to advanced analytics and automation tools, AI has permeated various aspects of the business world, transforming industries and redefining how we work.

The emergence of AI in the business world can be traced back to the mid-20th century when computer scientists and mathematicians began exploring the idea of creating machines that could mimic human intelligence. This pursuit led to the development of early AI systems, such as the General Problem Solver and ELIZA, which laid the foundation for future advancements in the field. However, it was only with the advent of the internet and the exponential growth of computing power that AI became a disruptive force in the business landscape.

In recent years, the rapid advancements in AI technologies, such as machine learning, natural language processing, and computer vision, have enabled businesses to harness the power of AI to streamline operations, enhance decision-making, and drive innovation. The proliferation of big data has further accelerated the adoption of AI, as organizations now have access to vast amounts of information that can be analyzed and leveraged to gain valuable insights and improve business outcomes.

As AI continues to evolve, it is reshaping the business world in several ways. For instance, AI-powered automation is transforming how businesses manage their supply chains, optimize logistics, and handle customer service. In addition, AI-driven analytics enables organizations to make data-driven decisions, identify trends, and uncover hidden patterns that can lead to new opportunities and competitive advantages.

Moreover, AI is also playing a crucial role in developing innovative products and services, as companies can now leverage AI technologies to create personalized experiences, enhance user engagement, and drive customer satisfaction. Furthermore, AI is fostering new business models and strategies, as organizations can now harness the power of AI to create value, differentiate themselves from competitors, and stay ahead of the curve in an increasingly competitive and dynamic business environment.

In conclusion, the emergence of AI in the business world has ushered in a new era of innovation, efficiency, and growth. As AI technologies advance and become more accessible, businesses across industries must adapt and embrace the AI revolution to stay relevant and thrive in the digital age. This book aims to empower managers with the knowledge and tools they need to navigate the AI landscape, harness its potential to drive success and create a future driven by artificial intelligence.

Empowering Managers to Navigate the AI Landscape

The dawn of the AI revolution has brought forth many opportunities and challenges for businesses across the globe. As managers, staying ahead of the curve and adapting to this rapidly evolving landscape is crucial. This book aims to empower you, the modern manager, with the knowledge and tools necessary to navigate the complex world of artificial intelligence.

In today's competitive business environment, relying solely on traditional management techniques is no longer enough. Integrating AI into various aspects of business operations has become necessary for organizations seeking to maintain a competitive edge. This book aims to comprehensively understand AI fundamentals, its applications in the business world, and the strategies required for successful implementation.

By delving into the core concepts of AI, this book will enable managers to make informed decisions about adopting and integrating AI technologies within their organizations. Furthermore, it will provide insights into AI's ethical considerations and potential pitfalls, ensuring managers are well-equipped to address any challenges.

This book will engage readers and facilitate a deeper understanding of AI in management through a multifaceted approach that combines expository, descriptive, narrative, and persuasive writing styles. The narrative style will bring the concepts to life by presenting real-world examples and case studies. At the same time, the persuasive elements will encourage readers to embrace the potential of AI in their organizations.

In conclusion, this book aims to empower managers with the knowledge and confidence to navigate the AI landscape, ensuring that they are well-prepared for a future driven by artificial intelligence. By understanding the fundamentals of AI, its applications in the business world, and the strategies for successful implementation, managers will be better equipped to lead their organizations into the new era of AI-driven innovation.

From AI Fundamentals to Implementation Strategies

As we embark on this journey to explore the world of artificial intelligence, it is crucial to understand the scope of this book and how it aims to empower managers like you. Our goal is to provide a comprehensive guide that covers the fundamentals of AI and delves into practical implementation strategies that can be applied in various business contexts.

To begin with, we will lay the foundation by discussing AI's core concepts and principles. This includes an overview of its history, the different types of AI, and the underlying technologies that drive its development, such as machine learning, deep learning, and natural language processing. By grasping these essential concepts, you will be better equipped to appreciate the potential of AI and its relevance to your organization.

Next, we will explore the various applications of AI across different industries and business functions. From marketing and customer service to finance and human resources, AI has the potential to revolutionize the way we work and make decisions. By examining real-world case studies and success stories, you will gain valuable insights into how AI can be harnessed to drive innovation, efficiency, and competitive advantage.

As a manager, it is vital to understand the ethical and legal implications of AI adoption. Therefore, we will dedicate a section discussing the potential risks, challenges, and ethical considerations of integrating AI into your business operations. This will enable you to make informed decisions and ensure that your organization complies with relevant regulations and industry standards.

Once you understand the AI landscape, we will delve into the practical aspects of implementing AI in your organization. This includes identifying the right AI solutions for your business needs, building a robust AI strategy, and managing the change process effectively. We will also discuss the importance of fostering a culture of innovation and collaboration and developing the necessary skills and competencies within your team to harness the full potential of AI.

Finally, we will look toward the future and explore the emerging trends and developments in AI. By staying informed about the latest advancements and anticipating the potential impact on your industry, you can position your organization at the forefront of the AI revolution and ensure long-term success.

In conclusion, this book aims to provide a multifaceted approach to AI in management, equipping you with the knowledge, tools, and strategies necessary to navigate the rapidly evolving AI landscape. By embracing the power of artificial intelligence, you can unlock new opportunities, drive innovation, and lead your organization into a future driven by AI.

Preparing for a Future Driven by Artificial Intelligence

As we stand on the precipice of a new era in business, it is crucial for managers to not only understand the transformative power of artificial intelligence but also embrace it wholeheartedly. The AI revolution is upon us, rapidly reshaping how we work, communicate, and make decisions. In this ever-evolving landscape, managers well-versed in AI fundamentals and implementation strategies will be better equipped to lead their organizations into a prosperous and innovative future.

Throughout this book, we have explored the various facets of AI, delving into its history, current applications, and potential to revolutionize industries across the globe. We have also examined the challenges and ethical considerations of integrating AI into the workplace. By providing a comprehensive and multifaceted approach to AI in management, this book aims to empower managers with the knowledge and tools necessary to navigate the complex world of artificial intelligence.

As we move forward, managers need to remain adaptable and open-minded, embracing the potential of AI to enhance their decision-making processes, streamline operations, and foster a culture of innovation within their organizations. By doing so, they will be better prepared to face the challenges of an increasingly competitive business environment and seize the opportunities that AI presents.

In conclusion, the future of business is undeniably intertwined with the advancements in artificial intelligence. As managers, we are responsible for staying informed, adapting, and leading our teams through this transformative period. By embracing the AI revolution and harnessing its potential, we can ensure that our organizations thrive in the dynamic and exciting world that lies ahead.

1

UNDERSTANDING ARTIFICIAL INTELLIGENCE: KEY CONCEPTS AND TERMINOLOGY

A digital brain with glowing circuits, surrounded by floating holographic screens displaying binary code and AI algorithms, set against a backdrop of deep space.

I n today's rapidly evolving technological landscape, artificial intelligence (AI) has emerged as a driving force behind innovation and progress in various industries. As a manager, it is crucial to stay informed and knowledgeable about AI, as it has the potential to revolutionize the way businesses operate and compete in the global market. This chapter aims to comprehensively understand AI, its key concepts, and terminology, enabling managers to make informed decisions and effectively integrate AI into their business strategies.

The importance of AI knowledge for managers cannot be overstated. As AI advances and becomes more integrated into our daily lives, managers need to understand its potential applications and implications. This understanding will not only help managers identify opportunities for AI implementation but also enable them to address potential challenges and ethical considerations that may arise.

Moreover, having a solid grasp of AI concepts and terminology will empower managers to communicate effectively with technical teams and make informed decisions when investing in AI technologies. This knowledge will also help managers to stay ahead of the curve, as they will be better equipped to anticipate and adapt to the ever-changing AI landscape.

This chapter will provide a comprehensive overview of artificial intelligence, exploring its origins, development, and current state. Next, we will delve into the key AI concepts, such as machine learning, deep learning, and neural networks, which form the foundation of modern AI systems. To ensure that managers are well-versed in the technical jargon associated with AI, we will also provide a guide to essential AI terminology.

Finally, we will examine real-world applications of AI, showcasing how it transforms business operations across various industries. By the end of this chapter, managers will have a solid understanding of AI and its potential impact on their organizations, enabling them to embrace AI and confidently prepare for the future.

Defining Artificial Intelligence: A Comprehensive Overview

In today's rapidly evolving technological landscape, artificial intelligence (AI) has emerged as a game-changing force, revolutionizing how businesses operate and managers make decisions. But what exactly is AI, and how can we define it in a way that is both comprehensive and accessible to managers? In this section, we will delve into the fascinating world of AI, providing a clear and concise overview of its core principles and components.

At its most fundamental level, artificial intelligence refers to developing computer systems that can perform tasks that typically require human intelligence. These tasks include learning, reasoning, problem-solving, perception, and understanding natural language. The ultimate goal of AI is to create machines that can think, learn, and adapt independently, thereby enhancing human capabilities and improving our ability to solve complex problems.

To better understand AI, it is helpful to break it down into two main categories: narrow AI and general AI. Narrow AI, or weak AI, refers to systems designed to perform specific tasks without possessing true intelligence or consciousness. Examples of narrow AI include speech recognition software, recommendation algorithms, and autonomous vehicles. These systems are highly specialized and excel at their designated tasks, but they lack the ability to think or reason beyond their programming.

On the other hand, general AI, or strong AI, refers to systems that possess human-like intelligence and can perform any intellectual task that a human being can do. While this level of AI remains a theoretical concept, it represents the ultimate aspiration of AI researchers and developers. Achieving general AI would mean creating machines that can perform tasks and understand and reason about the world in the same way humans do.

Now that we have a basic understanding of AI let's explore some key concepts underpinning its development and functionality. In the next section, we will delve into the fascinating realms of machine learning, deep learning, and neural networks, shedding light on the mechanisms that enable AI systems to learn and adapt over time. By grasping these foundational concepts, managers will be better equipped to harness the power of AI in their organizations and navigate the challenges and opportunities that this transformative technology presents.

Key AI Concepts: Machine Learning, Deep Learning, and Neural Networks

As a manager, it is crucial to have a solid understanding of the key concepts that underpin artificial intelligence. This will not only help you make informed decisions but also enable you to communicate effectively with your technical team. This section will delve into three fundamental AI concepts: machine learning, deep learning, and neural networks.

Machine Learning: Teaching Computers to Learn

At the heart of artificial intelligence lies machine learning, a subset of AI that focuses on developing algorithms and statistical models that enable computers to learn from and make predictions or decisions based on data. In other words, machine learning allows computers to identify patterns and trends without being explicitly programmed to do so.

There are three main types of machine learning:

- **Supervised Learning:** In this approach, the algorithm is trained on a labeled dataset, which means that the input data is paired with the correct output. The algorithm learns to map inputs to outputs and can then make predictions on new, unseen data.
- **Unsupervised Learning:** Unlike supervised learning, unsupervised learning deals with unlabeled data. The algorithm must identify patterns and relationships within the data with guidance on the output. This is often used

for tasks such as clustering and dimensionality reduction.

- **Reinforcement Learning:** This type of learning is inspired by how humans and animals learn from their environment. The algorithm learns by interacting with its environment and receiving feedback through rewards or penalties. The goal is to maximize the cumulative reward over time.

Deep Learning: Unleashing the Power of Neural Networks

Deep learning is a more advanced subset of machine learning that utilizes artificial neural networks to model and solve complex problems. These networks mimic how the human brain processes information, allowing computers to recognize patterns and make decisions with minimal human intervention.

The term "deep" refers to the multiple layers of interconnected nodes or neurons within the network. Each layer is responsible for processing different aspects of the input data, and the depth of the network allows it to learn more abstract and complex features.

Neural Networks: The Building Blocks of Deep Learning

Neural networks are the foundation of deep learning and consist of interconnected nodes or neurons that process and transmit information. These networks are organized into layers, each receiving input from the previous one and passing its output to the next.

There are three main types of layers in a neural network:

- **Input Layer:** This is the first layer of the network and is responsible for receiving the raw data. Each node in this layer represents a single input data feature or attribute.
- **Hidden layer(s):** These are the layers between the input and output layers. They perform complex computations and transformations on the input data, allowing the network to learn abstract features and representations.

- **Output Layer:** The final layer of the network produces the output or prediction based on the processed input data. The number of nodes in this layer depends on the problem being solved, such as the number of classes in a classification task.

In conclusion, understanding these key AI concepts - machine learning, deep learning, and neural networks - is essential for managers who wish to harness the power of artificial intelligence in their organizations. By grasping these fundamental ideas, you will be better equipped to make informed decisions, communicate with your technical team, and ultimately drive your business forward in the rapidly evolving world of AI.

Essential AI Terminology: A Manager's Guide to Technical Jargon

As a manager, it is crucial to have a firm grasp of the key terms and concepts related to artificial intelligence. This understanding will not only help you communicate effectively with your technical team but also enable you to make informed decisions about AI implementation in your organization. This section will explore some of the most important AI terminology that every manager should be familiar with.

- **Algorithm:** An algorithm is a set of rules or instructions a computer follows to solve a problem or complete a task. In AI, algorithms process data, identify patterns, and make predictions or decisions based on that data.
- **Supervised Learning:** This is a type of machine learning where the algorithm is trained on a labeled dataset, which means that the input data is paired with the correct output. The algorithm learns from this data and then applies it to new, unlabeled data.
- **Unsupervised Learning:** Unlike supervised learning, unsupervised learning algorithms are not provided with

labeled data. Instead, they must independently identify patterns and relationships within the data. This type of learning is often used for tasks such as clustering and dimensionality reduction.

- **Reinforcement Learning:** In reinforcement learning, an AI agent learns by interacting with its environment and receiving feedback through rewards or penalties. The agent's goal is maximizing its cumulative reward over time, often involving learning an optimal strategy through trial and error.
- **Natural Language Processing (NLP):** NLP is a subfield of AI that focuses on enabling computers to understand, interpret, and generate human language. This technology is used in chatbots, sentiment analysis, and machine translation applications.
- **Computer Vision:** This is another subfield of AI that enables computers to interpret and understand visual information from the world, such as images and videos. Computer vision is used in facial recognition, object detection, and autonomous vehicles.
- **Neural Network:** A neural network is a machine learning model inspired by the human brain's structure and function. It consists of interconnected nodes or neurons that process and transmit information. Neural networks are particularly effective at handling complex tasks like image and speech recognition.
- **Deep Learning:** Deep learning is a subset of machine learning that involves training large neural networks with multiple layers. These deep neural networks can learn hierarchical representations of data, which allows them to excel at tasks such as image and speech recognition, natural language processing, and game playing.
- **Transfer Learning:** Transfer learning is a technique in which a pre-trained neural network is fine-tuned for a new

task or domain. This approach can save time and resources by leveraging the knowledge gained from previous training.

- **Bias and Fairness:** In the context of AI, bias refers to the presence of systematic errors in an algorithm's predictions, often stemming from biased training data. Fairness, on the other hand, is the equitable treatment of different groups by an AI system. Ensuring that AI systems are unbiased and fair is critical for managers implementing AI in their organizations.

In conclusion, understanding these essential AI terms and concepts will empower you as a manager to make informed decisions about AI implementation and effectively communicate with your technical team. By embracing AI and staying informed about its developments, you will be better prepared to lead your organization into the future.

Real-World Applications: How AI is Transforming Business Operations

As a manager, it is crucial to understand the practical applications of artificial intelligence (AI) in today's business landscape. By grasping the transformative power of AI, you can better position your organization for success and capitalize on the opportunities it presents. This section will explore some real-world applications of AI and how they revolutionize various aspects of business operations.

Customer Service and Support

One of the most visible applications of AI in business is using chatbots and virtual assistants to enhance customer service and support. These AI-powered tools can handle various tasks, from answering frequently asked questions to guiding customers through complex processes. By automating routine customer interactions, businesses can reduce response times, improve customer satisfaction, and free up human agents to focus on more complex issues.

Sales and Marketing

AI is also transforming the way businesses approach sales and marketing. Machine learning algorithms can analyze vast amounts of data to identify patterns and trends, enabling businesses to understand their customers better and target their marketing efforts more effectively. AI-powered tools can also help sales teams prioritize leads, predict customer behavior, and personalize their interactions, leading to increased sales and improved customer relationships.

Supply Chain Management

In supply chain management, AI is used to optimize logistics and streamline operations. Machine learning algorithms can analyze historical data to predict demand, allowing businesses to make more informed decisions about inventory levels and production schedules. AI can also help identify inefficiencies in the supply chain, such as bottlenecks or underutilized resources, enabling managers to make data-driven decisions that improve overall efficiency.

Human Resources

AI is making its mark on human resources (HR) by automating repetitive tasks and providing valuable insights into employee performance and engagement. AI-powered tools can help HR professionals sift through large numbers of job applications, identify top candidates, and predict which applicants are most likely to succeed in a given role. Additionally, AI can analyze employee feedback and sentiment, helping managers identify areas for improvement and fostering a more positive work environment.

Decision-Making and Strategy

Finally, AI plays an increasingly important role in decision-making and strategy development. Businesses can uncover hidden patterns and insights that inform strategic decisions by leveraging machine learning algorithms and advanced analytics. AI can also help managers simulate various scenarios and predict the potential outcomes of different strategies, enabling them to make more informed choices and better prepare for the future.

In conclusion, AI transforms business operations in many ways, from enhancing customer service to streamlining supply chain management. As a manager, embracing AI and understanding its potential applications within your organization is essential. By doing so, you can position your business for success and ensure you are prepared to navigate the rapidly evolving landscape of AI-driven innovation.

Embracing AI as a Manager and Preparing for the Future

As we reach the end of this enlightening journey through the world of artificial intelligence, it is crucial for managers to not only understand the key concepts and terminology but also to embrace AI and its potential impact on the future of business operations. In this concluding section, we will discuss the importance of adopting AI as a manager and outline the steps to prepare for the inevitable AI-driven future.

The rapid advancements in AI technology have made it an essential component of modern business strategies. As a manager, embracing AI means recognizing its potential to transform your organization and industry and actively seeking ways to integrate it into your operations. This proactive approach will help you stay ahead of the competition and ensure that your organization remains relevant and agile in the ever-evolving business landscape.

To prepare for the future, managers must take the following steps:

- **Stay informed:** Stay updated on AI trends, research, and developments. This will enable you to make informed decisions about adopting and implementing AI technologies in your organization.

- **Develop a strategic vision:** Identify the areas within your organization where AI can have the most significant impact and create a strategic vision for its integration. This vision should be aligned with your organization's overall goals and objectives.
- **Foster a culture of innovation:** Encourage a culture of innovation and experimentation within your organization. This will help your team members to be more open to new ideas and technologies, including AI.
- **Invest in education and training:** Ensure your team members have the skills and knowledge to use AI technologies. This may involve investing in training programs, workshops or even hiring AI experts to guide your team.
- **Collaborate with AI experts:** Establish partnerships with AI experts, researchers, and technology providers to gain insights into the latest AI developments and best practices. This will help you make informed decisions about adopting and implementing AI technologies in your organization.
- **Monitor and evaluate AI initiatives:** Regularly monitor and evaluate the performance of your AI initiatives to ensure that they deliver the desired results. This will help you identify areas that require improvement and adjust your AI strategy.

In conclusion, the future of business is undeniably intertwined with artificial intelligence. As a manager, it is your responsibility to embrace AI and prepare your organization for the inevitable changes it will bring. By staying informed, developing a strategic vision, fostering a culture of innovation, investing in education and training, collaborating with AI experts, and monitoring and evaluating AI initiatives, you will be well-equipped to navigate the challenges and opportunities presented by AI and lead your organization into a successful and prosperous future.

Chapter Summary

- Artificial intelligence (AI) is a driving force behind innovation and progress in various industries, making it crucial for managers to stay informed and knowledgeable about its potential applications and implications.
- AI can be categorized into narrow AI (weak AI) and general AI (strong AI), with narrow AI focusing on specific tasks without true intelligence or consciousness and general AI aiming to achieve human-like intelligence across all intellectual tasks.
- Key AI concepts include machine learning, deep learning, and neural networks, which form the foundation of modern AI systems and enable them to learn and adapt over time.
- Understanding essential AI terminology, such as supervised learning, unsupervised learning, reinforcement learning, natural language processing, and computer vision, is crucial for managers to make informed decisions and communicate effectively with technical teams.
- Real-world applications of AI are transforming business operations across various industries, including customer service, sales and marketing, supply chain management, human resources, and decision-making and strategy.
- Embracing AI as a manager involves recognizing its potential to transform organizations and industries, actively seeking ways to integrate it into operations, and staying informed about the latest AI trends and developments.
- Preparing for the AI-driven future requires developing a strategic vision for AI integration, fostering a culture of innovation, investing in education and training, collaborating with AI experts, and monitoring and evaluating AI initiatives.
- By understanding and embracing AI, managers can position their organizations for success, navigate the rapidly evolving

AI landscape, and lead their teams into a successful and prosperous future.

2

THE EVOLUTION OF AI: A BRIEF
HISTORY AND ITS IMPACT ON
BUSINESS

A visual journey of AI evolution, starting from an abacus, transforming into an old computer, then a modern laptop, and finally morphing into a futuristic neural network.

I n today's fast-paced world of technology, artificial intelligence (AI) has surfaced as a critical catalyst in the transformation of diverse industries. As companies aim to remain competitive and ahead of the game, it's essential to grasp the fundamentals of AI and its possible uses for effective management. This chapter thoroughly reviews AI's evolution, its influence on business procedures, and the potential future trends that managers need to be aware of.

The concept of AI has been around for decades, but only in recent years have we witnessed its true potential unfold. From automating mundane tasks to revolutionizing decision-making processes, AI has proven to be a game-changer in how businesses operate. As a manager, it is essential to recognize the value of AI and its potential to reshape the business landscape.

In the following sections, we will delve into the early beginnings of AI, exploring the pioneering concepts and visionaries that laid the foundation for this groundbreaking technology. We will then examine the AI boom, highlighting the technological advancements that have propelled AI into the forefront of business operations. Furthermore, we will discuss the modern era of AI, focusing on machine learning, deep learning, and their practical applications in various industries.

As we venture into the future of AI, we will explore emerging trends and their potential impacts on business strategies. By understanding the trajectory of AI's development and its implications for the business world, managers can better prepare themselves and their organizations for transformative changes.

In conclusion, this chapter will provide managers with a solid understanding of AI's history, current applications, and potential future developments. By embracing the AI revolution and staying informed about its progress, managers can ensure that their businesses remain agile, innovative, and ready to face the challenges of an increasingly AI-driven world.

The Dawn of Artificial Intelligence: Early Concepts and Pioneers

As we embark on this journey to explore the fascinating world of artificial intelligence (AI), it is essential to understand its origins and the visionaries who laid the groundwork for the AI revolution. The dawn of AI can be traced back to the mid-20th century when the concept of creating intelligent machines first captured the imagination of scientists, mathematicians, and philosophers.

The Birth of an Idea: Turing and the Turing Test

The story of AI begins with the brilliant British mathematician and logician Alan Turing. In 1950, Turing published a groundbreaking paper titled "Computing Machinery and Intelligence," he proposed a test to determine if a machine could exhibit intelligent behavior indistinguishable from that of a human. This test, now known as the Turing Test, laid the foundation for the field of AI and sparked a debate on the possibility of machine intelligence that continues to this day.

The Pioneers: McCarthy, Minsky, and the Birth of AI as a Discipline

The 1950s saw the emergence of several key figures who would shape the field of AI. Among them were John McCarthy, an American computer scientist, and Marvin Minsky, a cognitive scientist and co-founder of the Massachusetts Institute of Technology's (MIT) Media Lab. In 1956, McCarthy and Minsky, along with other leading researchers, organized the Dartmouth Conference, which marked the birth of AI as a distinct discipline. The conference aimed to explore the potential of machines to simulate various aspects of human intelligence, such as learning, problem-solving, and language understanding.

Early AI Programs: Chess, Language, and Problem Solving

The 1960s and 1970s witnessed the development of several early AI programs that demonstrated the potential of machines to perform tasks previously thought to be the exclusive domain of human intelligence. Among these were chess-playing programs, such as IBM's Deep Blue, which defeated the reigning world champion, Garry Kasparov, in 1997. Another notable example was SHRDLU, a natural language understanding program developed by Terry Winograd at MIT, which could interpret and respond to simple English sentences.

The AI Winter: Challenges and Lessons Learned

Despite these early successes, the field of AI faced significant challenges in the 1970s and 1980s as researchers grappled with the limitations of their approaches and the complexity of simulating human intelligence. Funding for AI research dwindled, and the field entered a period of stagnation known as the "AI winter." However, this period also provided valuable lessons and insights that would later contribute to the resurgence of AI in the 1990s and beyond.

In conclusion, the early days of AI were marked by groundbreaking ideas, pioneering researchers, and ambitious projects that sought to push the boundaries of what machines could achieve. While the path was not without its challenges, these early efforts laid the foundation for the future AI boom, transforming how businesses operate and setting the stage for a future where AI plays an increasingly central role in our lives.

The AI Boom: Technological Advancements and Their Influence on Business Operations

As the sun began to rise on the horizon of artificial intelligence, a new era of technological advancements emerged, casting a transformative light on the business world. As it came to be known, the AI boom was characterized by rapid innovation and the development of cutting-edge tools and techniques that would forever change how businesses operate. In this section, we will delve into the key milestones of the AI boom and explore how these breakthroughs have shaped the modern business landscape.

The Birth of Machine Learning: Paving the Way for AI in Business

The AI boom can be traced back to the advent of machine learning, a revolutionary approach to AI that enabled computers to learn from data and improve their performance over time. This groundbreaking concept was first introduced by Arthur Samuel in 1959, who demonstrated the potential of machine learning through a simple yet powerful example: a computer program that could teach itself to play checkers.

As machine learning algorithms grew more sophisticated, businesses began to recognize the immense value of harnessing this technology to optimize their operations. From predicting customer behavior to automating complex decision-making processes, machine learning opened the door to a new world of possibilities for businesses seeking a competitive edge.

The Rise of Deep Learning: Unleashing the Power of Neural Networks

The next major milestone in the AI boom came with the rise of deep learning, a subset of machine learning that leverages artificial neural networks to mimic the human brain's ability to process and interpret vast amounts of information. Pioneered by Geoffrey Hinton and his team in the late 2000s, deep learning has since become the driving force behind many of the most advanced AI applications in business today.

Deep learning has enabled businesses to tackle previously insurmountable challenges, such as image and speech recognition, natural language processing, and even original content creation. By harnessing the power of deep learning, businesses have streamlined their operations, enhanced their products and services, and delivered more personalized experiences to their customers.

AI in Action: Real-World Business Applications

The AI boom has given rise to many practical applications that have transformed how businesses operate across various industries. Some notable examples include:

- **Customer Service:** AI-powered chatbots and virtual assistants have revolutionized customer service by providing instant, personalized support, reducing response times, and freeing human agents to focus on more complex tasks.
- **Marketing and Sales:** AI-driven analytics and predictive modeling have enabled businesses to understand their customers better, tailor their marketing campaigns, and optimize their sales strategies.
- **Supply Chain Management:** AI has been instrumental in optimizing supply chain operations, from demand forecasting and inventory management to route optimization and quality control.
- **Human Resources:** AI has streamlined recruitment by automating candidate screening, skill assessment, and even conducting preliminary interviews.
- **Finance:** AI has enhanced financial decision-making through advanced risk assessment, fraud detection, and algorithmic trading.

The AI Boom: A Catalyst for Business Transformation

The AI boom has undoubtedly left an indelible mark on the business world, driving innovation and fostering a culture of continuous improvement. As AI technologies evolve, businesses must adapt and embrace these advancements to stay ahead of the curve and capitalize on the opportunities they present. By harnessing the power of AI, businesses can unlock new levels of efficiency, agility, and growth, paving the way for a brighter, more prosperous future.

AI in the Modern Era: Machine Learning, Deep Learning, and Business Applications

As we venture into the modern era of artificial intelligence, it is essential to understand the key concepts that have shaped the AI landscape and their implications for businesses. This section will delve into machine learning, deep learning, and their various applications in the business world.

Machine Learning: The Driving Force Behind AI

Machine learning, a subset of AI, has emerged as a game-changing technology that enables computers to learn from data and improve their performance over time. This is achieved through algorithms that iteratively learn from data, allowing the system to make predictions or decisions without being explicitly programmed.

In the business context, machine learning has opened up many opportunities for organizations to gain insights from vast amounts of data, automate processes, and enhance decision-making. Some common applications of machine learning in business include:

- **Customer segmentation:** By analyzing customer data, machine learning algorithms can identify patterns and group customers based on their preferences, behaviors, and demographics. This enables businesses to tailor their marketing strategies and improve customer engagement.
- **Fraud detection:** Machine learning can help businesses detect unusual patterns and anomalies in transactions, which may indicate fraudulent activities. This allows organizations to prevent financial losses and protect their reputation proactively.
- **Inventory management:** Machine learning can optimize inventory levels by predicting demand and identifying trends, ensuring businesses maintain the right stock to meet customer needs while minimizing costs.

Deep Learning: Taking AI to New Heights

Deep learning, a more advanced subset of machine learning, has further revolutionized the AI landscape. It involves using artificial neural networks inspired by the human brain's structure and function. These networks can process vast amounts of data and identify complex patterns, enabling machines to perform tasks that were once considered impossible for computers.

Deep learning has particularly succeeded in image and speech recognition, natural language processing, and autonomous vehicles. In the business world, deep learning has found applications in:

- **Sentiment analysis:** By analyzing text data from sources like social media, customer reviews, and emails, deep learning algorithms can determine the sentiment behind the text, allowing businesses to gauge customer satisfaction and respond accordingly.
- **Chatbots and virtual assistants:** Deep learning has enabled the development of more sophisticated chatbots and virtual assistants that can understand and respond to natural language queries, providing customers with personalized support and improving the overall customer experience.
- **Predictive maintenance:** Deep learning can analyze sensor data from equipment and machinery to predict potential failures, allowing businesses to schedule maintenance and avoid costly downtime.

Harnessing the Power of AI in Business

The modern era of AI, characterized by machine learning and deep learning, has created many opportunities for businesses to enhance operations, drive innovation, and gain a competitive edge. By understanding and embracing these technologies, organizations can unlock the full potential of AI and prepare for a transformative future.

In the next section, we will explore the emerging trends in AI and their potential impacts on business strategies, ensuring that managers are well-equipped to navigate the ever-evolving AI landscape.

The Future of AI: Emerging Trends and Potential Impacts on Business Strategies

As we venture into the uncharted territory of the future, artificial intelligence (AI) continues evolving at an unprecedented pace, shaping how businesses operate and strategize. In this section, we will explore the emerging trends in AI and their potential impacts on business strategies, providing managers with valuable insights to navigate the transformative landscape ahead.

The Rise of AI-Driven Decision Making

One of the most significant trends in AI is the increasing reliance on data-driven decision-making. As AI algorithms become more sophisticated, they can analyze vast amounts of data and generate actionable insights, enabling businesses to make informed decisions based on empirical evidence. This shift towards AI-driven decision-making will require managers to adapt their strategies, placing greater emphasis on data collection, analysis, and interpretation.

The Integration of AI Across Business Functions

As AI technologies become more accessible and affordable, businesses will increasingly integrate AI across various functions, from marketing and sales to human resources and customer service. This widespread adoption of AI will necessitate reevaluating traditional business processes, as managers must determine how to leverage AI best to streamline operations, enhance efficiency, and drive innovation.

The Emergence of AI Ethics and Regulations

As AI becomes more ingrained in our daily lives, ethical considerations and regulatory frameworks will play a crucial role in shaping the future of AI in business. Managers must stay informed about the evolving ethical and legal landscape surrounding AI, ensuring that their organizations adhere to best practices and comply with relevant regulations. This will involve developing robust AI governance structures and fostering a culture of ethical AI use within the organization.

The Growing Importance of AI Talent and Education

As AI transforms the business landscape, the demand for skilled AI professionals will grow exponentially. To stay competitive, businesses must invest in AI education and training, cultivating a workforce capable of harnessing the power of AI to drive growth and innovation. This may involve partnering with educational institutions, offering in-house training programs, or providing employees access to online resources and courses.

The Need for Human-AI Collaboration

While AI has the potential to automate many tasks, it is essential to recognize that human expertise and intuition remain invaluable assets in the business world. The future of AI in business will likely involve a symbiotic relationship between humans and machines, each complementing the other's strengths and weaknesses. Managers must balance AI-driven automation and human ingenuity, fostering a collaborative environment where both can thrive.

In conclusion, the future of AI presents both challenges and opportunities for businesses. By staying informed about emerging trends and adapting their strategies accordingly, managers can harness the power of AI to drive growth, innovation, and success in the ever-evolving business landscape. Embracing the AI revolution and preparing for a transformative future will be essential for businesses to remain competitive and thrive in the age of artificial intelligence.

Embracing the AI Revolution and Preparing for a Transformative Future

As we have journeyed through the fascinating evolution of artificial intelligence, it is evident that AI has come a long way since its early conceptualizations. From the pioneering work of Alan Turing and John McCarthy to the groundbreaking advancements in machine learning and deep learning, AI has transformed how businesses operate and strategize. As we stand on the cusp of a new era, managers must embrace the AI revolution and prepare for a transformative future.

The AI revolution is not a distant dream but a present reality. Companies across industries are harnessing the power of AI to streamline operations, enhance customer experiences, and gain a competitive edge. As a manager, it is essential to recognize the potential of AI in your organization and identify areas where it can be effectively implemented. This may involve investing in AI-driven tools and technologies, upskilling your workforce, or collaborating with AI experts to develop tailored solutions.

Embracing the AI revolution also requires a shift in mindset. Managers must be open to experimentation and willing to adapt to new working methods. This includes fostering a culture of innovation and encouraging employees to think creatively about how AI can be leveraged to solve complex business challenges. By nurturing an environment that embraces change, managers can ensure that their organizations remain agile and responsive to the ever-evolving AI landscape.

As we look to the future, it is clear that AI will continue to shape the world of business in profound ways. Emerging trends such as natural language processing, autonomous systems, and AI-driven decision-making will further revolutionize how companies operate and interact with their customers. To stay ahead of the curve, managers must proactively monitor these developments and assess their potential impact on business strategies.

In conclusion, the AI revolution presents immense business opportunities and challenges. By embracing this transformative technology and preparing for its future advancements, managers can position their organizations for success in the rapidly evolving world of AI. As we continue to witness the remarkable progress of artificial intelligence, it is crucial for managers not only to adapt but also to lead the way in shaping a future where AI and human ingenuity work hand in hand to drive growth, innovation, and prosperity.

Chapter Summary

- The concept of AI has been around for decades, but its true potential has only been realized in recent years, revolutionizing various industries and transforming business operations.
- The early days of AI were marked by groundbreaking ideas and pioneering researchers, laying the foundation for the AI boom that followed and changed the way businesses operate.
- Machine learning, a subset of AI, has enabled computers to learn from data and improve their performance over time, opening up numerous opportunities for businesses to optimize their operations.
- Deep learning, a more advanced subset of machine learning, has further revolutionized the AI landscape, enabling machines to perform tasks that were once considered impossible for computers.
- AI has found practical applications in various industries, such as customer service, marketing and sales, supply chain management, human resources, and finance.
- Emerging trends in AI, such as AI-driven decision-making, integration of AI across business functions, AI ethics and regulations, and the growing importance of AI talent and education, will shape the future of AI in business.

- The future of AI in business will likely involve a symbiotic relationship between humans and machines, each complementing the other's strengths and weaknesses.
- Embracing the AI revolution and preparing for a transformative future is essential for businesses to remain competitive and thrive in the age of artificial intelligence.

3
_____

AI TECHNOLOGIES: MACHINE LEARNING, DEEP LEARNING, AND NATURAL LANGUAGE PROCESSING

A futuristic computer lab with glowing blue neural networks visualizing machine learning processes.

I n today's rapidly evolving business landscape, artificial intelligence (AI) has emerged as a game-changing technology that is transforming how organizations operate and compete. As a manager, it is crucial to understand the basics of AI technologies and their potential applications in your industry. This chapter will provide a comprehensive overview of the key AI technologies, namely machine learning, deep learning, and natural language processing, and how they can be integrated into your business strategy.

AI technologies have the potential to revolutionize various aspects of management, from automating routine tasks and enhancing decision-making processes to improving customer experiences and driving innovation. By leveraging these cutting-edge tools, managers can unlock new opportunities for growth, efficiency, and competitive advantage.

To begin our exploration of AI technologies, let us first clearly understand what artificial intelligence is. At its core, AI refers to developing computer systems that can perform tasks that typically require human intelligence. These tasks include learning from experience, recognizing patterns, understanding natural language, and making decisions based on complex data.

Now that we have a foundational understanding of AI let us delve deeper into the three primary technologies that drive its capabilities: machine learning, deep learning, and natural language processing. Each of these technologies offers unique benefits and applications, and together, they form the backbone of AI's transformative potential in the management world.

Machine Learning: The Foundation of AI

As a manager, you may have heard the term "machine learning" thrown around in discussions about artificial intelligence. But what exactly is machine learning, and why is it considered the foundation of AI? This section will delve into the fascinating world of machine learning, explore its various types, and understand its significance in AI.

Machine learning is a subset of artificial intelligence that focuses on developing algorithms and statistical models that enable computers to learn and improve from experience without being explicitly programmed. In simpler terms, it is the process through which machines can analyze vast amounts of data, identify patterns, and make decisions or predictions based on that information.

There are three primary types of machine learning: supervised learning, unsupervised learning, and reinforcement learning. We've briefly discussed them in chapter one, but as each type has its unique approach to learning and problem-solving, we must go deeper.

- **Supervised Learning:** In supervised learning, the machine is provided with a labeled dataset, which means that the input data is paired with the correct output. The machine uses this dataset to learn the relationship between the input and output and then applies this knowledge to make predictions on new, unseen data. Supervised learning is commonly used in applications such as image recognition, speech recognition, and financial forecasting.
- **Unsupervised Learning:** Unlike supervised learning, unsupervised learning deals with unlabeled data. The machine finds patterns, relationships, or structures within the data without prior knowledge of the desired output. Unsupervised learning is often used for tasks such as clustering (grouping similar data points) and dimensionality reduction (reducing the number of variables in a dataset while preserving its essential information).
- **Reinforcement Learning:** Reinforcement learning is a unique approach to machine learning, where an agent learns to make decisions by interacting with its environment. The agent receives feedback through rewards or penalties and adjusts its actions accordingly to maximize the cumulative reward. This type of learning is beneficial in situations where the optimal solution is not known in

advance and must be discovered through trial and error, such as in robotics and game-playing.

Machine learning is often called the foundation of AI because it allows computers to learn, adapt, and evolve without human intervention. By harnessing the power of machine learning, AI systems can analyze vast amounts of data, uncover hidden patterns, and make predictions with remarkable accuracy. This ability to learn from data and improve over time is what sets AI apart from traditional rule-based systems. It has led to groundbreaking advancements in computer vision, natural language processing, and robotics.

In conclusion, machine learning is a crucial component of artificial intelligence that enables machines to learn from experience and make data-driven decisions. As a manager, understanding the basics of machine learning and its various types will help you appreciate the potential of AI technologies and make informed decisions about their implementation in your organization. The next section will dive deeper into AI by exploring deep learning and its transformative impact on neural networks.

Deep Learning: Unleashing the Power of Neural Networks

As a manager, you may have heard the term "deep learning" thrown around in discussions about artificial intelligence. But what exactly is deep learning, and how does it differ from machine learning? How can you harness its power to drive your business forward? This section will delve into the fascinating world of deep learning, explore its potential applications, and provide the knowledge you need to make informed decisions about incorporating this cutting-edge technology into your organization.

Deep learning is a subset of machine learning that uses artificial neural networks to process and analyze data. These networks are inspired by the structure and function of the human brain, with interconnected nodes or "neurons" working together to process information and generate insights. The term "deep" refers to the multiple layers of neurons that make up these networks, allowing them to learn and recognize complex patterns and relationships in the data.

While both machine learning and deep learning involve the use of algorithms to analyze data and make predictions, there are some key differences between the two. Traditional machine learning algorithms often require manual feature extraction, meaning that a human expert must identify and select the most relevant variables for the algorithm to consider. On the other hand, deep learning can automatically discover and extract relevant features from raw data, making it more efficient and less reliant on human intervention.

Another significant difference is the ability of deep learning models to handle unstructured data, such as images, audio, and text. Traditional machine learning algorithms typically struggle with this type of data, whereas deep learning models excel at identifying patterns and relationships within them. This makes deep learning particularly well-suited for tasks such as image recognition, natural language processing, and speech recognition.

The power of deep learning to process and analyze vast amounts of complex data has opened up a world of possibilities for businesses across various industries. Some of the most promising applications of deep learning include:

- **Customer segmentation:** By analyzing customer data, deep learning models can identify patterns and trends that help businesses better understand their target audience and tailor their marketing strategies accordingly.
- **Fraud detection:** Deep learning algorithms can quickly and accurately identify suspicious transactions or activities, helping businesses protect themselves from financial losses and maintain their reputation.
- **Product recommendation:** By analyzing customer preferences and purchase history, deep learning models can generate personalized product recommendations, increasing customer satisfaction and loyalty.

- **Predictive maintenance:** Deep learning can analyze sensor data from equipment and machinery to predict when maintenance is needed, reducing downtime and increasing operational efficiency.
- **Sentiment analysis:** Deep learning models can gauge public sentiment towards a brand or product by processing and analyzing customer reviews and social media posts. This allows businesses to make data-driven decisions about their marketing and public relations strategies.

As a manager, it's essential to recognize the potential of deep learning and consider how it can be integrated into your organization's strategy. Begin by identifying areas where deep learning could have the most significant impact, such as improving customer service, streamlining operations, or enhancing product offerings. Next, collaborate with your IT and data teams to assess your organization's current infrastructure and determine the resources needed to implement deep learning solutions. Finally, consider partnering with AI and deep learning experts to ensure your organization is leveraging the latest advancements in this rapidly evolving field.

In conclusion, deep learning represents a powerful tool for businesses looking to harness the full potential of artificial intelligence. By understanding the basics of deep learning and its applications, you, as a manager, can make informed decisions about incorporating this technology into your organization's strategy and embracing the future of AI in management.

Natural Language Processing: Bridging the Gap Between Humans and Machines

As we delve deeper into artificial intelligence, managers must understand the significance of Natural Language Processing (NLP) and its potential impact on businesses. NLP, a subfield of AI, focuses on the interaction between humans and computers through natural language. In simpler terms, it enables machines to understand, interpret, and generate human language in a meaningful and useful way. This section will provide an overview of NLP, its applications, and how it can be integrated into your business strategy.

Understanding Natural Language Processing

At its core, NLP aims to bridge the gap between human communication and computer understanding. It involves various techniques and algorithms that allow machines to process and analyze large volumes of text or speech data. This is achieved by breaking down sentences into words, phrases, or symbols and then analyzing their structure, meaning, and context. By doing so, NLP enables computers to extract valuable insights and information from unstructured data, such as emails, social media posts, customer reviews, and more.

Applications of Natural Language Processing

NLP has various applications across various industries, making it an essential tool for businesses leveraging AI technologies. Some of the most common applications include:

- **Sentiment Analysis:** By analyzing the sentiment behind customer feedback, businesses can gain valuable insights into their products and services, allowing them to make data-driven decisions and improve customer satisfaction.
- **Chatbots and Virtual Assistants:** NLP-powered chatbots and virtual assistants can understand and respond to customer queries in real time, providing personalized support and enhancing the overall customer experience.
- **Text Classification:** NLP can be used to categorize and organize large volumes of text data, such as emails, documents, or articles, making it easier for businesses to manage and access information.

- **Machine Translation:** NLP enables translating text or speech from one language to another, breaking down language barriers and facilitating global communication.
- **Speech Recognition:** By converting spoken language into written text, NLP allows for voice-activated commands, transcription services, and more.

Integrating NLP into Your Business Strategy

To harness the power of NLP, managers must first identify the areas within their business where language processing can provide the most value. This may involve analyzing customer feedback, streamlining communication channels, or automating routine tasks. Once the potential applications have been identified, businesses can explore various NLP tools and platforms available in the market or even consider developing custom solutions tailored to their needs.

In conclusion, Natural Language Processing is a powerful AI technology that has the potential to revolutionize the way businesses interact with their customers, employees, and data. By understanding the basics of NLP and its applications, managers can make informed decisions on how to integrate this technology into their business strategy, ultimately driving growth and success in the age of AI.

Integrating AI Technologies into Your Business Strategy

As a manager, understanding the potential of AI technologies is only the first step in harnessing their power for your organization. The real challenge lies in effectively integrating machine learning, deep learning, and natural language processing into your business strategy. This section will explore the key considerations and best practices for incorporating AI technologies into your organization's operations and decision-making processes.

Identify the right opportunities

Before diving into AI implementation, it is crucial to identify the areas within your organization where AI technologies can have the most significant impact. Start by analyzing your business processes, customer interactions, and data management systems to pinpoint areas that could benefit from automation, enhanced decision-making, or improved efficiency. Some common use cases for AI technologies include customer service, fraud detection, marketing, and supply chain optimization.

Develop a clear AI strategy

Once you have identified the opportunities for AI integration, develop a comprehensive AI strategy outlining your organization's goals, objectives, and desired outcomes. This strategy should include an AI implementation roadmap detailing the necessary resources, timelines, and milestones. It is also essential to establish a system for measuring the success of your AI initiatives, using key performance indicators (KPIs) that align with your organization's overall objectives.

Assemble a cross-functional AI team

Successful AI integration requires collaboration between various departments and stakeholders within your organization. Assemble a cross-functional team that includes representatives from IT, data science, business operations, and other relevant departments. This team will oversee the AI implementation process, ensuring all stakeholders are aligned and working towards the same goals.

Invest in the right infrastructure and tools

Implementing AI technologies requires a robust infrastructure that can handle the demands of data processing, storage, and analysis. Invest in the necessary hardware, software, and cloud-based solutions to support your AI initiatives. Additionally, ensure your organization can access the right tools and platforms for machine learning, deep learning, and natural language processing, such as TensorFlow, Keras, and NLTK.

Foster a culture of AI adoption

For AI technologies to truly transform your organization, fostering a culture of AI adoption among your employees is essential. Encourage a mindset of continuous learning and innovation, providing training and resources to help your team members understand and embrace AI technologies. Empowering your employees to leverage AI in their daily tasks and decision-making processes can drive greater efficiency, productivity, and overall success for your organization.

Monitor, evaluate, and iterate

AI integration is an ongoing process that requires continuous monitoring, evaluation, and iteration. Regularly assess the performance of your AI initiatives, using the KPIs established in your AI strategy to determine their effectiveness. Be prepared to make adjustments and improvements as needed, ensuring that your AI technologies continue to deliver value and drive positive outcomes for your organization.

In conclusion, integrating AI technologies into your business strategy is a complex but rewarding endeavor. By identifying the right opportunities, developing a clear AI strategy, assembling a cross-functional team, investing in the necessary infrastructure and tools, fostering a culture of AI adoption, and continuously monitoring and iterating, you can unlock the full potential of AI for your organization and embrace the future of AI in management.

Embracing the Future of AI in Management

As we reach the end of this enlightening journey through the world of artificial intelligence, managers need to recognize the transformative potential of AI technologies in business. Machine learning, deep learning, and natural language processing are not just buzzwords or fleeting trends; they are powerful tools that can revolutionize the way organizations operate, compete, and thrive in an increasingly digital and data-driven world.

The key to harnessing the full potential of AI lies in understanding its capabilities and limitations and developing a strategic approach to its implementation. Managers must be proactive in staying informed about the latest advancements in AI technologies and be prepared to adapt their business strategies accordingly. This requires a willingness to embrace change, invest in continuous learning, and foster a culture of innovation within the organization.

One of the most critical aspects of integrating AI technologies into your business strategy is identifying the areas where these tools can have the most significant impact. This may involve automating repetitive tasks, enhancing decision-making processes, or improving customer experiences. By pinpointing the specific challenges that AI can help address, managers can ensure that their investments in these technologies yield tangible results and drive long-term growth.

Moreover, managers must recognize that successfully implementing AI technologies goes beyond merely acquiring the right tools and software. It also involves cultivating the necessary skills and expertise within the organization. This may entail hiring new talent, upskilling existing employees, or partnering with external experts to bridge knowledge gaps. By fostering a workforce well-versed in AI, managers can ensure that their organizations are well-equipped to navigate the complexities of this rapidly evolving landscape.

Finally, it is essential for managers to approach the integration of AI technologies with a sense of responsibility and ethical awareness. As powerful as these tools may be, they have risks and challenges. Issues such as data privacy, algorithmic bias, and the potential displacement of human workers must be carefully considered and addressed to ensure that the adoption of AI technologies is both sustainable and socially responsible.

In conclusion, the future of AI in management is undoubtedly bright, filled with opportunities for growth, innovation, and competitive advantage. By embracing these technologies with a strategic, informed, and responsible approach, managers can lead their organizations into a new digital transformation and success era. The time to act is now – the future of AI is already here, and it is up to today's leaders to seize the moment and shape the course of their organizations for years to come.

Chapter Summary

- Artificial intelligence (AI) technologies, including machine learning, deep learning, and natural language processing, can revolutionize various management aspects and drive innovation, efficiency, and competitive advantage.
- Machine learning is a subset of AI that focuses on developing algorithms and statistical models that enable computers to learn and improve from experience without being explicitly programmed.
- Deep learning is a subset of machine learning that uses artificial neural networks to process and analyze data, excelling at identifying patterns and relationships within unstructured data such as images, audio, and text.
- Natural Language Processing (NLP) is a subfield of AI that enables machines to understand, interpret, and generate human language in a meaningful and useful way, with applications such as sentiment analysis, chatbots, and machine translation.
- To integrate AI technologies into a business strategy, managers should identify the right opportunities, develop a clear AI strategy, assemble a cross-functional AI team, invest in the necessary infrastructure and tools, and foster a culture of AI adoption.
- Continuous monitoring, evaluation, and iteration are essential for successful AI integration, ensuring that AI technologies continue to deliver value and drive positive outcomes for the organization.

- Cultivating the necessary skills and expertise within the organization is crucial for successful AI implementation, which may involve hiring new talent, upskilling existing employees, or partnering with external experts.
- Managers should approach the integration of AI technologies with a sense of responsibility and ethical awareness, addressing issues such as data privacy, algorithmic bias, and the potential displacement of human workers to ensure sustainable and socially responsible adoption.

4

THE ROLE OF DATA IN AI: COLLECTION, PROCESSING, AND ANALYSIS

A neon matrix of flowing data streams in a dark cybernetic environment.

I n today's swiftly changing business environment, artificial intelligence (AI) has surfaced as a revolutionary technology that is reshaping how organizations function and make choices. As a manager, comprehending the essential role of data in creating and applying AI solutions is vital. This chapter intends to offer an all-inclusive review of the importance of data in AI and how managers can utilize its potential to propel innovation and success within their organizations.

Data is often called the "fuel" that powers AI systems. Without data, AI algorithms would be unable to learn, adapt, and improve their performance over time. Data serves as the raw material that AI systems use to identify patterns, make predictions, and generate insights that can inform strategic decision-making. As a manager, recognizing the value of data in AI initiatives is the first step toward unlocking the full potential of this transformative technology.

The process of leveraging data in AI projects can be broadly divided into three main stages: data collection, data processing, and data analysis. Each stage plays a critical role in ensuring the success of AI-driven solutions and requires careful planning and execution.

In the following sections, we will delve deeper into the various strategies and techniques involved in data collection, processing, and analysis and how they can be effectively integrated into management practices. By gaining a solid understanding of these concepts, managers will be better equipped to make informed decisions about AI projects and ensure that their organizations remain at the forefront of innovation.

As we explore the world of data and its role in AI, it is important to remember that the ultimate goal is to create value for your organization. By embracing data-driven AI solutions and fostering a culture of continuous learning and improvement, managers can unlock new opportunities for growth and success in an increasingly competitive business environment.

Data Collection: Strategies and Techniques for AI Projects

In today's rapidly evolving business landscape, the ability to harness the power of artificial intelligence (AI) is no longer a luxury but a necessity for managers. One of the most critical aspects of AI implementation is data collection, as it forms the foundation upon which AI systems are built and trained. In this section, we will explore various strategies and techniques for data collection that can help managers successfully integrate AI into their projects.

Identifying Data Needs

Before diving into data collection, it is essential for managers to identify the specific data needs of their AI projects. This involves determining the type of data required, the volume of data needed, and the desired level of data quality. By clearly defining these parameters, managers can ensure their data collection efforts are targeted and efficient.

Primary and Secondary Data Sources

Data collection can be broadly categorized into two types: primary and secondary. Primary data refers to information that is collected directly from the source, such as through surveys, interviews, or observations. Conversely, secondary data is information that has already been collected and is available for use, such as existing databases, reports, or research studies. Managers should consider primary and secondary data sources when planning their AI projects, as each offers unique advantages and limitations.

Data Collection Techniques

Numerous data collection techniques are available to managers, each with its own set of benefits and drawbacks. Some of the most common techniques include:

- **Surveys and Questionnaires:** These tools allow managers to gather large amounts of data quickly and cost-effectively. However, they may be subject to biases and inaccuracies if not designed and administered properly.
- **Interviews:** Conducting one-on-one or group interviews can provide rich, in-depth insights into a particular topic. However, this method can be time-consuming and may not be feasible for large-scale data collection efforts.
- **Observations:** By observing and recording events or behaviors, managers can collect data that is free from the biases that may be present in self-reported data. However, this method can be labor-intensive and require specialized training to ensure accurate and consistent data collection.
- **Web Scraping:** This technique involves extracting data from websites and online sources, making it an excellent option for quickly collecting large volumes of data. However, web scraping may raise ethical and legal concerns, and the data quality may vary.

Ensuring Data Quality

Data quality is a crucial factor in the success of AI projects, as poor-quality data can lead to inaccurate or unreliable AI models. Managers should implement quality control measures throughout the data collection process, such as validating data sources, using standardized data collection tools, and regularly reviewing and cleaning the data.

Ethical Considerations

In addition to ensuring data quality, managers must also consider the ethical implications of their data collection efforts. This includes obtaining informed consent from participants, protecting the privacy and confidentiality of the data, and adhering to relevant laws and regulations.

In conclusion, data collection is a vital component of AI projects, and managers must carefully plan and execute their data collection efforts to ensure the success of their AI initiatives. By understanding the various strategies and techniques available and the importance of data quality and ethical considerations, managers can confidently navigate the complex world of AI data collection and lay the groundwork for AI-driven success in their organizations.

Data Processing: Preparing and Cleaning Data for AI Systems

In the world of artificial intelligence, data is the lifeblood that fuels the decision-making capabilities of AI systems. As a manager, understanding the process of data preparation and cleaning is crucial to ensure the success of AI projects within your organization. In this section, we will delve into the importance of data processing, the steps involved in preparing and cleaning data, and the role managers play in overseeing this critical aspect of AI implementation.

Data processing is transforming raw data into a structured format that AI systems can easily understand and analyze. This step is essential because AI algorithms rely on clean, accurate, and well-organized data to make informed decisions and predictions. Only accurate or complete data can lead to better decision-making, reduced efficiency, and even financial losses for your organization. As a manager, you are responsible for ensuring that the data used in AI projects is of the highest quality and has undergone thorough processing.

- **Data Exploration:** The first step in data processing is to explore the raw data and understand its structure, content, and potential issues. This involves examining the data's format, identifying missing or inconsistent values, and assessing the overall quality of the data.
- **Data Cleaning:** Once the data has been explored, the next step is to clean it by addressing any inconsistencies, errors, or missing values. This may involve correcting typos, filling in missing data points, or removing duplicate entries. Data cleaning is an iterative process, and it may require multiple

rounds of review and correction to ensure the data is accurate and consistent.

- **Data Transformation:** After cleaning the data, it must be transformed into a format that AI algorithms can easily understand. This may involve converting data types, scaling or normalizing values, or encoding categorical variables into numerical values. Data transformation ensures that AI systems can effectively analyze and interpret data.
- **Feature Engineering:** The final step in data processing is feature engineering, which involves selecting the most relevant variables or attributes from the data to be used as input for AI algorithms. This may involve creating new variables, combining existing variables, or reducing the dimensionality of the data. Feature engineering is crucial for improving the performance and accuracy of AI systems.

As a manager, your role in the data processing stage of AI projects is to oversee and guide the process, ensuring that the data is accurate, consistent, and well-structured. This may involve:

- Collaborating with data scientists and engineers to establish data processing goals and strategies.
- Allocating resources and setting timelines for data processing tasks.
- Monitoring the progress of data processing and addressing any issues or challenges that arise.
- Ensuring data processing meets industry standards, legal requirements, and ethical guidelines.
- Evaluating the quality of processed data and making informed decisions about its suitability for AI projects.

In conclusion, data processing is a critical aspect of AI implementation that managers must understand and oversee. Ensuring that your organization's data is properly prepared and cleaned can lay the foundation for successful AI projects that drive efficiency, innovation, and growth. Embrace the power of data and harness its potential to transform your management practices and elevate your organization's performance.

Data Analysis: Extracting Insights and Patterns for AI Decision-Making

In artificial intelligence, data is the lifeblood that fuels the decision-making process. As a manager, understanding the role of data analysis in AI is crucial to harnessing its full potential and driving your organization toward success. This section will explore the data analysis process, exploring how insights and patterns can be extracted to inform AI decision-making.

Data analysis examines, cleans, transforms, and models data to extract valuable information, draw conclusions, and support decision-making. In the context of AI, data analysis is essential for identifying patterns and trends that can be used to train and improve machine learning models. The primary goal of data analysis in AI is to uncover hidden relationships and insights that can be leveraged to make better decisions and predictions.

Several techniques and tools are used in data analysis, which can be broadly categorized into descriptive and predictive analytics.

Descriptive Analytics: This type of analysis focuses on summarizing and understanding the past. It involves the use of historical data to identify patterns, trends, and relationships that can provide insights into the current state of a business or system. Descriptive analytics techniques include data visualization, summary statistics, and clustering. These methods help managers understand the underlying structure of their data and identify areas of interest or concern.

Predictive Analytics: On the other hand, predictive analytics uses historical data to make predictions about future events or outcomes. This type of analysis is particularly relevant to AI, as it involves the use of machine learning algorithms to identify patterns and relationships in data that can be used to make informed decisions. Predictive analytics techniques include regression analysis, classification, and time series forecasting. These methods enable managers to anticipate future trends, identify potential risks, and make data-driven decisions that can improve the performance of their AI systems.

As a manager, it is essential to recognize the importance of data analysis in the AI decision-making process. By extracting insights and patterns from your data, you can better understand the factors influencing your organization's performance and make more informed decisions. Furthermore, data analysis can help you identify areas where AI can be most effectively applied, allowing you to prioritize resources and maximize the impact of your AI initiatives.

In conclusion, data analysis is a critical component of AI decision-making, providing the foundation for informed, data-driven decisions that can drive your organization toward success. By embracing the power of data analysis and incorporating it into your management practices, you can unlock the full potential of AI and position your organization for a successful future in the rapidly evolving world of artificial intelligence.

Implementing Data-Driven AI Solutions in Management Practices

In today's rapidly evolving business landscape, managers must be agile and adaptive to stay ahead of the curve. One of the most effective ways to achieve this is by implementing data-driven AI solutions in management practices. By leveraging the power of AI, managers can make more informed decisions, optimize processes, and drive innovation. This section will explore the key steps to integrate data-driven AI solutions into your management practices successfully.

- **Identify the problem or opportunity:** The first step in implementing AI solutions is clearly defining the problem or opportunity you wish to address. This could include improving customer satisfaction, streamlining supply chain operations, or enhancing employee productivity. You can better tailor your AI solution to meet your organization's needs by identifying the specific issue.

- **Set clear objectives:** Once you have identified the problem or opportunity, it is crucial to establish clear objectives for your AI project. These objectives should be SMART (Specific, Measurable, Achievable, Relevant, and Time-bound) to ensure your AI solution is focused and results-driven.
- **Assemble a cross-functional team:** Implementing AI solutions requires collaboration between various departments, including IT, data science, and business operations. By assembling a cross-functional team, you can ensure that all relevant stakeholders are involved in the decision-making process and that your AI solution is aligned with your organization's overall strategy.
- **Collect and process data:** As discussed in previous sections, data is the lifeblood of AI systems. To implement a successful AI solution, you must collect and process relevant data from various sources, such as customer interactions, internal databases, and external data providers. This data should be cleaned, organized, and transformed into a format that AI algorithms can easily analyze.
- **Develop and train AI models:** With your data, your team can now develop AI models tailored to your specific objectives. These models should be trained and tested using your processed data to ensure they can accurately predict outcomes, identify patterns, and make recommendations.
- **Integrate AI solutions into existing processes:** Once your AI models have been developed and tested, it is time to integrate them into your existing management practices. This may involve updating your software systems, retraining employees, or redefining workflows to accommodate the new AI-driven insights.
- **Monitor and evaluate performance:** After implementing your AI solution, it is essential to continuously monitor its performance and evaluate its impact on your organization. This will allow you to identify areas for improvement, fine-

tune your AI models, and ensure that your AI solution remains effective and relevant in the face of changing business conditions.

- **Foster a data-driven culture:** Finally, to fully reap the benefits of AI in management practices, fostering a data-driven culture within your organization is crucial. This involves promoting data literacy, encouraging data-driven decision-making, and investing in ongoing AI education and employee training.

In conclusion, implementing data-driven AI solutions in management practices can significantly improve efficiency, decision-making, and innovation. By following the steps outlined above, managers can successfully integrate AI into their organizations and harness the power of data to drive business success.

Embracing Data as the Foundation of AI Success in Management

In conclusion, data plays a pivotal role in successfully implementing artificial intelligence (AI) in management practices. As managers, understanding the significance of data collection, processing, and analysis is crucial in harnessing the full potential of AI to drive business growth and enhance decision-making processes. By embracing data as the foundation of AI success, managers can unlock new opportunities and stay ahead of the competition in today's rapidly evolving business landscape.

Throughout this chapter, we have explored the various aspects of data management in AI projects, from the strategies and techniques employed in data collection to preparing and cleaning data for AI systems. We have also delved into the importance of data analysis in extracting valuable insights and patterns that can inform AI-driven decision-making. By mastering these essential data management components, managers can ensure that their AI initiatives are built on a solid foundation.

Implementing data-driven AI solutions in management practices requires a shift in mindset and a willingness to adapt to new technologies. Managers must be open to learning and embracing the power of AI, as well as fostering a culture of innovation and collaboration within their teams. By doing so, they can create an environment where AI can thrive and deliver tangible results for the organization.

Moreover, managers need to stay informed about the latest AI and data management developments, as the field is constantly evolving. By staying up-to-date with the latest trends and best practices, managers can ensure that their AI initiatives remain relevant and effective in addressing the challenges faced by their organizations.

In summary, the role of data in AI cannot be overstated. By embracing data as the foundation of AI success in management, managers can unlock the full potential of AI to drive business growth, enhance decision-making processes, and stay ahead of the competition. As the world continues to embrace AI and its transformative capabilities, managers need to understand and harness the power of data to ensure the success of their AI initiatives.

Chapter Summary

- Data is the lifeblood of AI systems, serving as the raw material that AI algorithms use to identify patterns, make predictions, and generate insights for strategic decision-making.
- The process of leveraging data in AI projects involves three main stages: data collection, data processing, and data analysis, each playing a critical role in the success of AI-driven solutions.
- Data collection strategies and techniques include identifying data needs, using primary and secondary data sources, employing various data collection methods, ensuring data quality, and considering ethical implications.

- Data processing involves preparing and cleaning data for AI systems, including exploration, data cleaning, transformation, and feature engineering.
- Data analysis in AI focuses on extracting insights and patterns from data using descriptive and predictive analytics techniques, which help inform AI decision-making.
- Implementing data-driven AI solutions in management involves identifying problems or opportunities, setting clear objectives, assembling cross-functional teams, collecting and processing data, developing and training AI models, integrating AI solutions into existing processes, monitoring and evaluating performance, and fostering a data-driven culture.
- Embracing data as the foundation of AI success in management enables managers to unlock new opportunities, drive business growth, and stay ahead of the competition.
- Staying informed about the latest developments in AI and data management is crucial for managers to ensure that their AI initiatives remain relevant and effective in addressing their organization's challenges.

5

IMPLEMENTING AI IN BUSINESS: IDENTIFYING OPPORTUNITIES AND CHALLENGES

A futuristic office with AI robots performing business tasks under soft white lighting.

A rtificial intelligence (AI) has emerged as a game-changing force in today's rapidly evolving technological landscape, revolutionizing how businesses operate and compete. As a manager, it is crucial to understand the potential of AI and how it can be harnessed to drive innovation, efficiency, and growth within your organization. This chapter provides a comprehensive overview of the opportunities and challenges associated with implementing AI in business management, offering valuable insights and practical guidance for those seeking to embrace this transformative technology.

The AI revolution is already well underway, with companies across industries leveraging machine learning, natural language processing, and other AI technologies to streamline processes, enhance decision-making, and deliver more personalized customer experiences. From automating routine tasks to uncovering hidden patterns in vast datasets, AI enables businesses to operate more intelligently and effectively than ever.

However, the journey to AI-driven success has its challenges. Managers must navigate a complex landscape of technological, organizational, and ethical considerations to integrate AI into their business operations successfully. This requires a clear understanding of the potential benefits and risks associated with AI and a strategic approach to implementation that ensures alignment with broader business objectives.

In this chapter, we will explore how AI can transform your business, highlighting key opportunities for innovation and growth. We will also delve into the common challenges faced by organizations seeking to adopt AI, offering practical advice on overcoming these hurdles and maximizing the value of your AI investments. Through real-world case studies, we will demonstrate the power of AI in driving tangible business results, showcasing the successes of companies that have effectively harnessed this technology. Finally, we will outline best practices for AI integration and adoption, equipping you with the knowledge and tools needed to prepare for a future driven by AI in business management.

By understanding the fundamentals of AI and its potential applications in the business world, managers can position themselves at the forefront of this technological revolution, unlocking new growth and competitive advantage opportunities. Embracing AI in business management is no longer a choice but a necessity for those seeking to thrive in today's increasingly digital and data-driven landscape.

Identifying Opportunities: How AI Can Transform Your Business

As we explore the potential of artificial intelligence (AI) in business management, it is crucial to identify the opportunities that AI presents. By understanding how AI can transform your business, you can make informed decisions and strategically integrate AI solutions to enhance efficiency, productivity, and overall success.

Streamlining Operations and Enhancing Efficiency

One of AI's most significant opportunities is the ability to streamline operations and enhance efficiency. By automating repetitive tasks and processes, AI can free up valuable time and resources, allowing your team to focus on the business's more strategic and creative aspects. For instance, AI-powered chatbots can handle routine customer inquiries, while machine learning algorithms can optimize supply chain management by predicting demand patterns and identifying potential bottlenecks.

Data-Driven Decision Making

In today's data-driven world, businesses generate and collect vast information. AI can help managers make sense of this data by identifying patterns, trends, and insights that would otherwise remain hidden. Managers can make more informed decisions by leveraging AI-powered analytics tools, leading to improved business outcomes. For example, AI can help identify customer preferences and trends, enabling businesses to tailor their products and services better to meet customer needs.

Enhancing Customer Experience

AI has the potential to revolutionize the way businesses interact with their customers. By utilizing AI-powered tools such as chatbots, virtual assistants, and personalized recommendations, businesses can provide a more seamless and engaging customer experience. This improves customer satisfaction, fosters brand loyalty, and drives long-term growth.

Fostering Innovation and Creativity

AI can help businesses unlock their creative potential by automating routine tasks and providing valuable insights. With more time and resources, teams can focus on developing innovative products, services, and strategies that set them apart from the competition. Furthermore, AI can also assist in the creative process, offering suggestions and ideas based on data analysis and pattern recognition.

Expanding Market Reach

AI can help businesses expand their market reach by identifying new customer segments, untapped markets, and emerging trends. By leveraging AI-powered market research tools, businesses can gain a competitive edge and capitalize on new growth opportunities.

In conclusion, the opportunities presented by AI in business management are vast and varied. Businesses can transform their operations, enhance efficiency, and drive innovation by identifying these opportunities and strategically implementing AI solutions. In the following sections, we will delve deeper into the challenges of AI implementation and explore real-world examples of AI success in business management.

Overcoming Challenges: Addressing Common AI Implementation Hurdles

As businesses integrate AI into their operations, they will encounter various challenges. While the potential benefits of AI are immense, managers must be aware of these hurdles and develop strategies to overcome them. This section will discuss some of the most common challenges faced during AI implementation and provide practical solutions to address them.

Data Quality and Availability

One of the most significant challenges in implementing AI is data availability and quality. AI systems rely heavily on data to learn and make decisions. Therefore, it is essential to have access to accurate, relevant, and up-to-date data. To overcome this challenge, businesses should invest in robust data management systems and establish processes to ensure data quality and integrity. Additionally, collaborating with external data providers and leveraging open data sources can help enrich the available data pool.

Talent Acquisition and Retention

The demand for AI professionals, such as data scientists and machine learning engineers, has skyrocketed in recent years. Consequently, businesses face difficulties finding and retaining the right talent to develop and maintain AI systems. To address this challenge, organizations should invest in training and upskilling their existing workforce and partnering with academic institutions and research organizations to tap into a broader talent pool. Offering competitive compensation packages and fostering a culture of innovation can also help attract and retain top AI talent.

Integration with Existing Systems

Integrating AI solutions with existing business systems and processes can be complex and time-consuming. To ensure seamless integration, managers should involve all relevant stakeholders in the planning and implementation process, including IT teams, business analysts, and end-users. Adopting a modular and scalable approach to AI implementation can also help businesses gradually incorporate AI into their operations without disrupting existing workflows.

Ethical and Legal Considerations

AI systems can raise ethical and legal concerns like data privacy, algorithmic bias, and transparency. Managers should proactively address these concerns by establishing ethical guidelines for AI development and usage, conducting regular audits of AI systems, and ensuring compliance with relevant laws and regulations. Engaging with external experts and participating in industry forums can also help businesses stay informed about emerging ethical and legal issues related to AI.

Managing Expectations

Lastly, managers must manage expectations around AI implementation. While AI can benefit businesses significantly, it is not a magic solution that can solve all problems instantly. Managers should set realistic goals and timelines for AI projects and communicate them clearly to all stakeholders. By doing so, they can avoid disappointment and ensure that the organization remains committed to the long-term success of AI initiatives.

In conclusion, overcoming the challenges associated with AI implementation requires strategic planning, effective communication, and continuous learning. By addressing these hurdles head-on, businesses can successfully harness the power of AI to drive innovation and growth in their operations.

Case Studies: Real-World Examples of AI Success in Business Management

In this section, we will delve into real-world examples of how AI has been successfully implemented in various industries, showcasing the transformative power of this technology in business management. These case studies will provide valuable insights into the practical applications of AI, demonstrating how businesses have overcome challenges and reaped the benefits of AI integration.

Retail: Personalized Shopping Experiences with AI

One of the most prominent examples of AI success in business management can be found in the retail industry. E-commerce giant Amazon has been at the forefront of AI adoption, utilizing machine learning algorithms to analyze customer data and provide personalized product recommendations. This has not only improved customers' shopping experience but has also increased sales and customer loyalty. Similarly, clothing retailer Stitch Fix employs AI-powered algorithms to analyze customer preferences and deliver personalized clothing selections, resulting in higher customer satisfaction and retention rates.

Healthcare: Improved Diagnostics and Treatment Plans

AI has made significant strides in the healthcare industry, particularly in diagnostics and treatment planning. IBM's Watson, a powerful AI system, has assisted doctors in diagnosing and treating various medical conditions. By analyzing vast amounts of medical data, Watson can provide accurate diagnoses and recommend personalized treatment plans, leading to better patient outcomes. Additionally, AI-powered tools like Zebra Medical Vision's imaging analytics platform have been instrumental in detecting diseases such as cancer at early stages, enabling timely intervention and potentially saving lives.

Finance: Enhanced Fraud Detection and Risk Management

The finance industry has also embraced AI to improve its operations, particularly in fraud detection and risk management. Financial institutions like JPMorgan Chase and American Express have implemented AI-powered systems to analyze transaction data and identify patterns indicative of fraudulent activity. This has resulted in a significant reduction in financial losses due to fraud. Furthermore, AI-driven risk assessment tools have enabled banks and investment firms to make more informed decisions, leading to better portfolio management and increased returns on investment.

Manufacturing: Streamlined Production Processes and Quality Control

AI has revolutionized manufacturing by streamlining production processes and enhancing quality control measures. For instance, General Electric has employed AI-powered robots to inspect and repair jet engines, reducing inspection times by over 50% and minimizing human error. Similarly, Siemens has implemented AI-driven systems to optimize its production lines, increasing efficiency and reducing waste. These examples demonstrate how AI can significantly improve operational efficiency and product quality in the manufacturing sector.

Customer Service: AI-Powered Chatbots and Virtual Assistants

AI has also significantly impacted customer service with the advent of AI-powered chatbots and virtual assistants. Companies like Microsoft and Google have developed sophisticated AI systems that can understand and respond to customer queries in real time, providing quick and accurate assistance. This has improved customer satisfaction and reduced the workload on human customer service representatives, allowing them to focus on more complex tasks.

In conclusion, these case studies demonstrate the transformative potential of AI in various industries, highlighting the benefits of AI integration in business management. By learning from these real-world examples, managers can identify AI implementation opportunities in their organizations and develop strategies to overcome challenges and ensure successful AI adoption.

Best Practices: Strategies for Effective AI Integration and Adoption

As businesses increasingly embrace the potential of artificial intelligence (AI) to transform their operations, it is crucial to adopt best practices that ensure the successful integration and adoption of AI technologies. This section will explore strategies to help managers implement AI effectively in their organizations while minimizing potential risks and maximizing benefits.

Develop a Clear AI Strategy and Vision

Before embarking on the AI journey, it is essential for managers to have a clear understanding of their organization's goals and objectives in adopting AI technologies. This involves identifying the specific business problems that AI can help solve and the desired outcomes and key performance indicators (KPIs) that will be used to measure success. By establishing a well-defined AI strategy and vision, managers can ensure that their AI initiatives are aligned with the organization's overall business objectives and can effectively communicate the value of AI to stakeholders.

Foster a Culture of Innovation and Collaboration

Successful AI integration requires a culture encouraging innovation, experimentation, and collaboration. Managers should promote a mindset of continuous learning and improvement, where employees are encouraged to explore new ideas, share their knowledge, and work together to solve complex problems. This can be achieved through regular training sessions, workshops, and team-building activities that foster a sense of camaraderie and shared purpose. By creating an environment that supports innovation and collaboration, organizations can more effectively harness the power of AI to drive business growth.

Invest in Talent and Skills Development

As AI technologies evolve, organizations must invest in developing their workforce's skills and expertise. This includes hiring and retaining top talent in AI-related fields and providing ongoing training and development opportunities for existing employees. Managers should also consider partnering with educational institutions, industry associations, and other organizations to access specialized AI training programs and resources. By investing in talent and skills development, businesses can ensure they have the necessary expertise to implement AI technologies and stay ahead of the competition.

Establish Robust Data Management Practices

AI technologies rely heavily on data to function effectively, making it essential for organizations to have robust data management practices in place. This includes ensuring that data is accurate, complete, and up-to-date and implementing strong data security measures to protect sensitive information. Managers should also consider adopting data governance frameworks and tools that can help streamline data management processes and ensure compliance with relevant regulations. By establishing solid data management practices, organizations can maximize the effectiveness of their AI initiatives and minimize potential risks.

Monitor and Evaluate AI Performance

To ensure the ongoing success of AI initiatives, managers need to monitor and evaluate AI technologies' performance regularly. This involves tracking the progress of AI projects against predefined KPIs and conducting regular audits and assessments to identify areas for improvement. Managers should also be prepared to adjust their AI strategy and implementation plans as needed based on the insights gained from performance monitoring and evaluation. By maintaining a proactive approach to AI performance management, organizations can ensure their AI initiatives continue delivering value and driving business growth.

In conclusion, the successful integration and adoption of AI technologies in business management require a strategic approach, a culture of innovation and collaboration, investment in talent and skills development, robust data management practices, and ongoing performance monitoring and evaluation. By adopting these best practices, managers can effectively harness the power of AI to transform their organizations and prepare for a future driven by AI in business management.

Preparing for a Future Driven by AI in Business Management

As we conclude this enlightening journey through artificial intelligence and its impact on business management, we must reflect on the key takeaways and prepare ourselves for the inevitable AI-driven future. The transformative power of AI is undeniable, and as managers, it is our responsibility to harness this potential to drive innovation, efficiency, and growth in our organizations.

First and foremost, it is crucial to recognize that AI is not a fleeting trend or a mere buzzword; it is a powerful tool that is here to stay and will continue to revolutionize how we conduct business. Embracing the AI revolution means acknowledging its potential and proactively seeking opportunities to integrate AI into various aspects of your organization. This may include automating repetitive tasks, enhancing decision-making processes, or creating new products and services.

Identifying these opportunities requires a keen understanding of your organization's unique needs and challenges and a willingness to think creatively and strategically about how AI can address them. It is essential to stay informed about the latest advancements in AI technology and to collaborate with experts in the field to ensure that your organization remains at the forefront of innovation.

However, implementing AI in business management has its challenges. As with any significant change, there will be hurdles to overcome, such as addressing concerns about job displacement, ensuring data privacy and security, and navigating the complexities of AI integration. By anticipating and proactively addressing these challenges, managers can mitigate potential risks and create a smoother transition to an AI-driven business model.

The case studies presented in this chapter are powerful examples of how AI can be successfully integrated into various industries and business functions. By examining these real-world applications, managers can gain valuable insights into the strategies and best practices that have led to AI success. These lessons can then be applied to your organization, helping to guide your AI implementation journey.

In conclusion, the future of business management is undeniably intertwined with the advancements in artificial intelligence. As managers, we must prepare for this future by embracing AI, identifying opportunities for its integration, and overcoming the challenges that may arise along the way. By doing so, we can ensure that our organizations remain competitive, innovative, and poised for success in the rapidly evolving landscape of AI-driven business management.

Chapter Summary

- AI has the potential to revolutionize business management by streamlining operations, enhancing efficiency, fostering innovation, and improving customer experiences.
- Identifying opportunities for AI integration requires a clear understanding of an organization's unique needs and challenges and staying informed about the latest advancements in AI technology.
- Implementing AI in business management comes with challenges, such as data quality and availability, talent acquisition and retention, integration with existing systems, ethical and legal considerations, and managing expectations.
- Real-world case studies demonstrate the transformative potential of AI in various industries, highlighting the

benefits of AI integration in business management and providing valuable insights into practical applications.

- Best practices for effective AI integration and adoption include developing a clear AI strategy and vision, fostering a culture of innovation and collaboration, investing in talent and skills development, establishing robust data management practices, and monitoring and evaluating AI performance.
- Overcoming the challenges associated with AI implementation requires strategic planning, effective communication, and continuous learning.
- Preparing for a future driven by AI in business management involves embracing AI, identifying opportunities for its integration, and overcoming the challenges that may arise along the way.
- The future of business management is undeniably intertwined with the advancements in artificial intelligence, and managers must adapt to ensure their organizations remain competitive, innovative, and poised for success in the rapidly evolving landscape of AI-driven business management.

6

AI ETHICS AND RESPONSIBLE MANAGEMENT: ENSURING FAIRNESS, TRANSPARENCY, AND ACCOUNTABILITY

A digital scale balancing a human brain and a circuit board, symbolizing AI ethics, under soft blue lighting.

A rtificial intelligence (AI) has surfaced as a potent instrument for revolutionizing how businesses function and decide in the swiftly changing tech world today. As AI systems increasingly become a part of diverse management facets, managers must comprehend the ethical consequences of these technologies and embrace responsible practices to guarantee fairness, transparency, and accountability. This chapter offers a detailed review of AI ethics and responsible management, emphasizing the significance of these principles in the successful execution and management of AI systems.

AI ethics refers to the moral principles and guidelines that govern the design, development, and deployment of AI technologies. These principles are essential in addressing AI's potential risks and unintended consequences, such as biased decision-making, lack of transparency, and misuse of personal data. On the other hand, responsible management involves adopting ethical practices and policies for managers to ensure that AI systems are used in a manner that aligns with the organization's values and societal norms.

As AI continues to permeate various industries and sectors, managers must have the knowledge and skills to navigate the complex ethical landscape surrounding these technologies. This chapter will delve into the importance of fairness in AI decision-making, highlighting the need for unbiased algorithms and data sets to prevent discriminatory outcomes. We will also explore the concept of transparency in AI systems and processes, emphasizing the significance of clear communication and understanding of AI's inner workings for managers and stakeholders.

Furthermore, this chapter will discuss the critical aspect of accountability in AI implementation and management, outlining managers' responsibilities in ensuring that AI systems are used ethically and in compliance with relevant regulations. To provide a comprehensive understanding of these concepts, we will also present real-world examples and case studies of ethical AI management, showcasing the challenges and successes experienced by organizations in various industries.

In conclusion, this chapter will offer a glimpse into the future of AI ethics and responsible management, highlighting the potential developments and challenges as AI continues to revolutionize how we live and work. By understanding and embracing these ethical principles, managers can harness the power of AI to drive innovation and growth while ensuring that their organizations remain committed to upholding the highest standards of fairness, transparency, and accountability.

Understanding the Importance of Fairness in AI Decision-Making

In today's rapidly evolving technological landscape, artificial intelligence (AI) has become an essential tool for businesses and organizations across various industries. As AI systems grow in complexity and capability, managers must understand the importance of fairness in AI decision-making. This section will delve into fairness, its significance in AI applications, and the potential consequences of biased AI systems.

Defining Fairness in AI

Fairness in AI refers to an AI system's equitable treatment of all individuals and groups, ensuring that its decisions do not discriminate against any particular demographic. This involves carefully considering various factors, such as race, gender, age, and socio-economic status, to guarantee that AI algorithms do not perpetuate existing biases or create new ones.

The Significance of Fairness in AI Applications

The importance of fairness in AI decision-making cannot be overstated. As AI systems become more integrated into our daily lives, they have the potential to significantly impact various aspects of society, from employment and education to healthcare and criminal justice. Ensuring fairness in AI applications is vital for several reasons:

- **Social Responsibility:** As managers, we are responsible for ensuring that the AI systems we implement do not perpetuate harmful biases or contribute to social inequality. By prioritizing fairness in AI decision-making, we can work towards creating a more just and equitable society.
- **Legal Compliance:** Many countries have enacted laws and regulations to prevent discrimination in various aspects of life. Fairness in AI systems can help organizations avoid legal repercussions and maintain a positive reputation.
- **Customer Trust:** Fair and unbiased AI systems can help build trust with customers and stakeholders as they demonstrate a commitment to ethical practices and social responsibility.

Consequences of Biased AI Systems

Ignoring the importance of fairness in AI decision-making can lead to severe consequences for individuals and organizations. Biased AI systems can:

- **Reinforce Stereotypes:** AI systems relying on biased data or algorithms can perpetuate harmful stereotypes, further marginalizing disadvantaged groups.
- **Limit Opportunities:** Unfair AI systems can restrict access to essential services, such as employment, education, and healthcare, for certain demographics.
- **Damage Reputation:** Organizations that employ biased AI systems may face public backlash, leading to a loss of trust and potential boycotts.
- **Legal Repercussions:** Companies that fail to ensure fairness in their AI systems may face legal penalties for discrimination, resulting in financial losses and damage to their reputation.

In conclusion, understanding the importance of fairness in AI decision-making is crucial for managers navigating the complex world of AI integration. By prioritizing fairness and working to eliminate biases in AI systems, managers can ensure that their organizations remain socially responsible, legally compliant, and trusted by customers and stakeholders.

Promoting Transparency and Ensuring Accountability in AI Systems and Processes

In today's rapidly evolving technological landscape, artificial intelligence (AI) has become integral to various industries, transforming how businesses operate and make decisions. As AI continues to permeate our daily lives, managers must understand the importance of promoting transparency and ensuring accountability in AI systems and processes. This section will delve into the concepts of transparency and accountability, their significance in AI, and practical steps managers can take to ensure that AI systems are transparent, accountable, and easily understandable.

Transparency in AI refers to the ability to understand and interpret the inner workings of an AI system, including its decision-making processes, algorithms, and data inputs. A transparent AI system allows users, stakeholders, and regulators to gain insights into how the system operates, the rationale behind its decisions, and the potential biases that may be present. On the other hand, accountability in AI systems refers to the ability to trace and explain the decision-making processes of AI algorithms and hold individuals and organizations responsible for the outcomes of these decisions.

Promoting transparency and ensuring accountability in AI systems and processes are essential for several reasons. Both foster trust between AI systems and their users, promote ethical decision-making and help organizations comply with regulations. Understanding the inner workings of an AI system allows managers to identify areas for improvement, leading to more accurate and efficient AI-driven processes.

Managers can take several practical steps to ensure transparency and accountability in their organization's AI systems. These include collaborating with AI developers, implementing explainable AI, documenting AI processes, conducting regular audits, and educating and training employees. Managers should also establish clear roles and responsibilities, implement robust documentation practices, conduct regular audits and reviews, and foster a culture of accountability within their organization.

Failing to promote transparency and ensure accountability in AI systems can have significant consequences for organizations, including loss of trust, legal and financial consequences, and ethical concerns. Therefore, it is critical to responsible AI management. By understanding the importance of transparency and accountability and taking practical steps, managers can build trust, ensure ethical decision-making, comply with regulations, and continuously improve their AI systems. As AI advances, transparency and accountability will remain vital to ethical and responsible AI management.

Real-World Examples and Case Studies of Ethical AI Management

This section will delve into real-world examples and case studies that demonstrate ethical AI management in action. These examples will provide valuable insights into how organizations can successfully implement AI systems while adhering to fairness, transparency, and accountability principles.

Google's AI Ethics Council

In 2019, Google established an AI Ethics Council to guide on ethical issues related to AI and other emerging technologies. The council, composed of experts from various fields, was tasked with ensuring that Google's AI projects align with the company's AI principles, which include being socially beneficial, avoiding unfair bias, and promoting transparency. Although the initial council faced some controversies and was eventually disbanded, Google's commitment to ethical AI management remains strong as they continue to seek external input and refine their approach to AI ethics.

IBM's AI Fairness 360 Toolkit

IBM has developed an open-source toolkit called AI Fairness 360, which provides a comprehensive set of metrics and algorithms to help organizations detect and mitigate bias in AI systems. The toolkit is designed to promote fairness in AI decision-making by enabling developers and data scientists to assess and improve their AI models throughout the development process. By making this toolkit available to the broader AI community, IBM demonstrates its commitment to fostering ethical AI management practices across the industry.

The Partnership on AI

The Partnership on AI is a collaborative initiative involving major tech companies, including Amazon, Apple, Google, Facebook, and Microsoft, as well as non-profit organizations and academic institutions. The partnership aims to develop best practices for AI ethics and promote transparency, fairness, and accountability in AI systems. Through research, public dialogue, and collaboration, the Partnership on AI seeks to address the global challenges posed by AI and ensure that AI technologies benefit all of humanity.

The European Union's AI Ethics Guidelines

In 2019, the European Union published AI ethics guidelines outlining key requirements for trustworthy AI systems. These guidelines emphasize the importance of human oversight, transparency, fairness, and accountability in AI development and deployment. By providing a clear framework for ethical AI management, the European Union aims to promote responsible AI innovation and ensure that AI technologies respect fundamental human rights and values.

The Case of Microsoft's Tay AI Chatbot

In 2016, Microsoft launched an AI chatbot named Tay, designed to learn from and engage with users on social media platforms. However, within hours of its release, Tay began to post offensive and inappropriate content, as it learned from the negative input it received from users. Microsoft quickly took Tay offline and apologized for the incident. This case study highlights the importance of ethical AI management, as it demonstrates the potential consequences of failing to consider AI systems' potential risks and biases.

In conclusion, these real-world examples and case studies illustrate the growing importance of ethical AI management in today's rapidly evolving technological landscape. By prioritizing fairness, transparency, and accountability, organizations can harness the power of AI while minimizing potential risks and ensuring that AI technologies serve the greater good. As AI continues to advance, managers must stay informed about ethical AI practices and actively work to promote responsible AI innovation within their organizations.

The Future of AI Ethics and Responsible Management

As we reach the end of our exploration into AI ethics and responsible management, it is crucial to reflect on the importance of these concepts in shaping the future of artificial intelligence. The rapid advancement of AI technologies has the potential to revolutionize various industries, streamline processes, and improve decision-making. However, without a strong ethical foundation and responsible management practices, these innovations may lead to unintended consequences, exacerbating existing inequalities and creating new ethical dilemmas.

The future of AI ethics and responsible management lies in managers, developers, policymakers, and other stakeholders, who must work together to ensure that AI systems are designed and implemented with fairness, transparency, and accountability at their core. By prioritizing these principles, organizations can harness the power of AI to drive positive change while minimizing the risks associated with its deployment.

One of the key challenges in achieving this goal is the need for continuous learning and adaptation. As AI technologies evolve, so must our understanding of their ethical implications and the best practices for managing them responsibly. This requires a commitment to ongoing education, collaboration, and dialogue among all stakeholders and the development of new tools and frameworks to guide ethical decision-making.

Moreover, the future of AI ethics and responsible management will depend on cultivating a diverse and inclusive workforce. By fostering a culture of diversity and inclusion, organizations can ensure that a wide range of perspectives and experiences are represented in the development and management of AI systems. This can help to identify and address potential biases, promote fairness, and enhance the overall effectiveness of AI technologies.

In addition to these efforts, the future of AI ethics and responsible management will be shaped by the emergence of new regulations and industry standards. Policymakers and industry leaders must work together to develop comprehensive guidelines that balance promoting innovation and protecting the rights and interests of individuals and communities affected by AI technologies. By establishing clear expectations and accountability mechanisms, these regulations can ensure that AI is used responsibly and ethically across all sectors.

Finally, the growing public awareness and engagement with AI-related issues will influence the future of AI ethics and responsible management. As more people become aware of AI's potential benefits and risks, they will play a critical role in holding organizations accountable for their actions and advocating for ethical AI practices. This increased public scrutiny will motivate organizations to prioritize ethical considerations in their AI strategies and decision-making processes.

In conclusion, AI ethics and responsible management future are promising and challenging. By embracing the principles of fairness, transparency, and accountability and fostering a culture of continuous learning, diversity, and public engagement, we can ensure that AI technologies are harnessed for the greater good. As managers, developers, policymakers, and citizens, we all have a role in shaping this future and creating a world where AI is a force for positive change rather than a source of harm or inequality.

Chapter Summary

- AI ethics and responsible management are crucial for ensuring fairness, transparency, and accountability in AI systems, which are increasingly integrated into various management and decision-making aspects.
- Fairness in AI decision-making involves treating all individuals and groups equitably, preventing biased algorithms and data sets from leading to discriminatory outcomes.
- Transparency in AI systems and processes is essential for building trust, ensuring ethical decision-making, maintaining compliance with regulations, and enabling continuous improvement.
- Accountability in AI implementation and management involves tracing and explaining AI decision-making processes and holding individuals and organizations responsible for the outcomes.
- Managers can promote ethical AI management by collaborating with developers, implementing explainable AI, documenting AI processes, conducting regular audits, and fostering a culture of accountability.
- Real-world examples and case studies, such as Google's AI Ethics Council and IBM's AI Fairness 360 Toolkit, demonstrate the importance of ethical AI management in practice.
- The future of AI ethics and responsible management depends on continuous learning, adaptation, diverse and

inclusive workforces, new regulations and industry standards, and increased public awareness and engagement.

- By embracing the principles of fairness, transparency, and accountability and fostering a culture of continuous learning, diversity, and public engagement, AI technologies can be harnessed for the greater good and serve as a force for positive change.

7

BUILDING AN AI-READY WORKFORCE: TALENT ACQUISITION, RETENTION, AND TRAINING

A futuristic AI training center with neon blue lights, holographic screens, and robots learning tasks.

Artificial intelligence (AI) has emerged as a game-changing force in today's rapidly evolving business landscape, revolutionizing how organizations operate and compete. As AI continues to permeate various industries, managers must stay ahead of the curve by understanding the implications of this transformative technology and preparing their workforce to harness its full potential. This chapter provides a comprehensive guide for managers seeking to build an AI-ready workforce, focusing on talent acquisition, retention, and training strategies.

The AI revolution is not a distant reality; it is happening now. From automating mundane tasks to making data-driven decisions, AI is transforming how businesses function and creating new opportunities for growth and innovation. As a manager, it is crucial to recognize the impact of AI on your organization and take proactive steps to adapt to this new paradigm.

Building an AI-ready workforce is more than hiring a few data scientists or software engineers. It involves creating a culture that embraces AI, fostering collaboration between technical and non-technical teams, and investing in continuously developing your employees' skills. By doing so, you will ensure that your organization remains competitive in the age of AI and empower your employees to thrive in this dynamic environment.

The following sections will delve deeper into the key aspects of building an AI-ready workforce, including identifying and attracting AI-proficient candidates, implementing effective retention strategies, and cultivating AI expertise within your organization. Additionally, we will discuss the role of managers in fostering an AI-driven culture and embracing the future of AI in workforce management.

As you embark on this journey, remember that the AI revolution presents an exciting opportunity for managers to redefine their roles and drive meaningful change within their organizations. By equipping your workforce with the right skills and mindset, you can unlock the true potential of AI and pave the way for a more efficient, innovative, and successful future.

Talent Acquisition: Identifying and Attracting AI-Proficient Candidates

The demand for AI-proficient candidates is skyrocketing in today's rapidly evolving technological landscape. As a manager, it is crucial to understand the importance of identifying and attracting top talent in artificial intelligence. This section will delve into the key aspects of talent acquisition, focusing on the strategies and techniques to help you build an AI-ready workforce.

The first step in acquiring AI-proficient talent recognizes the skills and qualifications essential for success in this field. Some of the most sought-after skills include:

- **Programming languages:** Proficiency in languages such as Python, R, and Java is crucial for AI development and implementation.
- **Machine learning and deep learning:** A strong foundation in these areas is vital for creating and refining AI algorithms.
- **Data analytics and visualization:** The ability to analyze and interpret large datasets is essential for AI-driven decision-making.
- **Problem-solving and critical thinking:** AI professionals must be able to think creatively and strategically to develop innovative solutions.
- **Communication and collaboration:** AI projects often involve cross-functional teams, making strong interpersonal skills necessary.

Once you clearly understand the skills and qualifications required for AI proficiency, the next step is to source potential candidates. Some effective strategies for finding top AI talent include:

- **Networking:** Attend industry conferences, workshops, and meetups to connect with AI professionals and expand your network.

- **Social media:** Use platforms like LinkedIn and Twitter to identify and engage with AI experts and enthusiasts.
- **Online communities:** Participate in AI-focused forums, discussion boards, and blogs to discover potential candidates and learn about their expertise.
- **Educational institutions:** Partner with universities and research institutions to tap into a pool of fresh talent and gain access to cutting-edge AI research.
- **Recruitment agencies:** Collaborate with specialized recruitment firms that focus on AI and technology to streamline your talent acquisition process.

You must differentiate your organization from the rest in a competitive job market. To attract top AI talent, consider the following strategies:

- **Showcase your commitment to AI:** Highlight your organization's dedication to AI innovation through case studies, whitepapers, and thought leadership content.
- **Offer competitive compensation and benefits:** Ensure that your compensation packages are on par with industry standards and offer unique benefits that cater to the needs of AI professionals.
- **Provide growth and development opportunities:** Demonstrate your commitment to employee growth by offering ongoing training, mentorship, and opportunities for advancement within the AI field.
- **Foster a culture of innovation:** Encourage creativity, experimentation, and collaboration by creating an environment where AI professionals can thrive.
- **Highlight your organization's social impact:** Showcase how your AI initiatives contribute to the greater good, as many AI professionals are driven by a desire to impact society positively.

By understanding the skills and qualifications of AI-proficient candidates, sourcing talent from the right channels, and creating a compelling employer brand, you can successfully build an AI-ready workforce that will drive your organization forward in the age of artificial intelligence.

Retention Strategies: Keeping Your AI-Savvy Workforce Engaged and Loyal

As the AI revolution continues to reshape the business landscape, managers must focus on acquiring top talent and retaining their AI-proficient workforce. In this section, we will explore various retention strategies to help managers keep their AI-savvy employees engaged, motivated, and loyal.

Recognizing and Rewarding AI Expertise

One of the most effective ways to retain AI-proficient employees is by recognizing and rewarding their expertise. Managers should establish a system that acknowledges the contributions of AI experts to the organization's success. This can be done through various means, such as offering promotions, bonuses, or other incentives that reflect the value of their skills and knowledge. By doing so, managers can demonstrate their appreciation for their AI-savvy workforce's hard work and dedication, fostering a sense of loyalty and commitment to the organization.

Providing Opportunities for Growth and Advancement

AI-proficient employees are often driven to learn and grow in their field. Managers can support this by providing ample opportunities for professional development and career advancement. This may include offering training programs, workshops, or conferences that allow employees to expand their AI knowledge and skills. Additionally, managers should encourage internal mobility, enabling AI experts to explore different organizational roles and responsibilities. By promoting a culture of continuous learning and growth, managers can ensure that their AI-savvy workforce remains engaged and motivated to excel in their careers.

Fostering a Collaborative and Supportive Work Environment

A supportive and collaborative work environment is crucial for retaining AI-proficient employees. Managers should encourage open communication and knowledge sharing among team members, promoting a culture of collaboration and innovation. This can be achieved by organizing regular team meetings, brainstorming sessions, or informal gatherings where employees can discuss their ideas, challenges, and successes. Moreover, managers should provide the necessary resources and tools that enable AI experts to work efficiently and effectively. By fostering a positive work environment, managers can help their AI-savvy workforce feel valued and supported, increasing job satisfaction and loyalty.

Ensuring Work-Life Balance

Work-life balance is essential to employee retention, particularly for those working in demanding fields such as AI. Managers should be mindful of their AI-proficient employees' workload and stress levels, ensuring they have the necessary support and resources to maintain a healthy work-life balance. This may include offering flexible work arrangements, such as remote work or flexible hours, and promoting a culture that values personal well-being and self-care. By prioritizing work-life balance, managers can help their AI-savvy workforce maintain a sustainable and fulfilling career within the organization.

In conclusion, retaining an AI-proficient workforce requires a multifaceted approach that addresses these talented individuals' unique needs and aspirations. By recognizing and rewarding their expertise, providing opportunities for growth and advancement, fostering a collaborative and supportive work environment, and ensuring work-life balance, managers can keep their AI-savvy employees engaged, motivated, and loyal to the organization. Embracing these retention strategies will benefit the employees and contribute to the organization's overall success and competitiveness in the rapidly evolving world of AI.

Training and Development: Cultivating AI Expertise Within Your Organization

As the world continues to embrace the transformative power of artificial intelligence (AI), organizations must invest in the training and development of their workforce. This ensures that employees are equipped with the necessary skills to navigate the AI landscape and fosters a culture of continuous learning and innovation. This section will delve into the importance of cultivating AI expertise within your organization and explore various strategies to achieve this goal.

The rapid advancements in AI technology have led to a growing demand for professionals with AI proficiency. By investing in the training and development of your workforce, you can ensure that your organization remains competitive in the ever-evolving AI landscape. Moreover, a well-trained workforce can increase productivity, improve decision-making, and enhance customer experiences.

Before embarking on the journey of AI training and development, it is essential to identify your organization's specific needs. This can be achieved by conducting a thorough skills gap analysis, which involves assessing the current AI capabilities of your workforce and comparing them with the desired level of expertise. This will help you pinpoint the areas where training is most needed and design targeted programs to address these gaps.

Once you have identified the AI training needs of your organization, the next step is to implement effective training programs. These can take various forms, such as workshops, seminars, online courses, and hands-on projects. It is important to choose the right mix of training methods that cater to your employees' diverse learning preferences and provide ample opportunities to apply their newly acquired skills in real-world scenarios.

In the fast-paced world of AI, fostering a culture of continuous learning within your organization is essential. This can be achieved by encouraging employees to stay updated on the latest AI trends and developments, providing access to relevant resources, and offering incentives for acquiring new skills. By promoting a growth mindset, you can ensure that your workforce remains agile and adaptable in the face of technological change.

To gauge the effectiveness of your AI training and development initiatives, it is crucial to establish key performance indicators (KPIs) and track them over time. These may include metrics such as employee engagement, skill acquisition, and the application of AI expertise in daily tasks. By regularly monitoring these KPIs, you can make data-driven decisions to refine your training programs and maximize their impact on your organization.

In conclusion, cultivating AI expertise within your organization is vital to building an AI-ready workforce. By identifying training needs, implementing targeted programs, fostering a culture of continuous learning, and measuring the impact of your initiatives, you can ensure that your employees are well-equipped to navigate the AI revolution and contribute to the success of your organization. As a manager, your role in this process is pivotal as you set the tone for a culture that embraces AI and encourages growth and innovation.

The Role of Managers in Fostering an AI-Driven Culture

As the world continues to embrace the transformative power of artificial intelligence (AI), managers must understand their role in fostering an AI-driven culture within their organizations. This section will delve into managers' responsibilities in cultivating an environment that encourages the adoption of AI technologies, promotes collaboration between AI and human talent, and supports continuous learning and innovation.

Managers play a pivotal role in driving the adoption of AI within their organizations. They must act as advocates for AI, educating their teams on the benefits and potential applications of these technologies. By clearly understanding AI's capabilities and limitations, managers can help dispel misconceptions and alleviate any fears or concerns that employees may have. This, in turn, will create a more receptive environment for AI integration and experimentation.

A successful AI-driven culture fosters collaboration between human and AI talent. Managers must work to break down silos and promote cross-functional teamwork, ensuring that employees with diverse skill sets and expertise can solve complex problems using AI. By encouraging open communication and knowledge sharing, managers can help their teams leverage the full potential of AI technologies and drive innovation.

As AI evolves rapidly, managers must prioritize continuous learning and professional development for their teams. This includes providing access to relevant training programs, workshops, and resources that can help employees stay up-to-date with AI advancements. Managers should also encourage their teams to experiment with new AI tools and techniques, fostering a culture of curiosity and innovation.

To further incentivize the adoption of AI, managers should recognize and reward employees who demonstrate exceptional AI-driven performance. This can include celebrating team successes, acknowledging individual contributions, and providing opportunities for career advancement within the organization. By recognizing and rewarding AI-driven success, managers can help reinforce the value of AI and motivate their teams to continue pushing the boundaries of what is possible with these technologies.

Finally, managers must lead by example, embracing AI and fostering an AI-driven culture. This means staying informed about the latest AI trends and developments, actively participating in AI-related initiatives, and demonstrating a willingness to adapt and evolve alongside these technologies. By embodying the principles of an AI-driven culture, managers can inspire their teams to follow suit and fully embrace the potential of AI in their work.

In conclusion, managers are critical in fostering an AI-driven culture within their organizations. By championing AI adoption, encouraging collaboration, supporting continuous learning, recognizing and rewarding AI-driven success, and leading by example, managers can help their organizations harness the power of AI and thrive in the rapidly evolving landscape of the digital age.

Embracing the Future of AI in Workforce Management

As we reach the end of our journey through the fascinating world of artificial intelligence and its impact on workforce management, it is essential to take a step back and reflect on the transformative power of this technology. The AI revolution is not a distant dream; it is happening now, and managers must be prepared to adapt and thrive in this new landscape. By focusing on talent acquisition, retention, and training, organizations can build an AI-ready workforce that will drive innovation and success in the future.

In this rapidly evolving environment, managers play a crucial role in fostering an AI-driven culture. They must be open to change, willing to learn, and proactive in seeking out opportunities to leverage AI for the betterment of their teams and organizations. This includes staying informed about the latest AI advancements, understanding the ethical implications of AI deployment, and promoting a culture of collaboration and continuous learning.

Embracing the future of AI in workforce management is challenging. Managers may face resistance from employees who fear job displacement or struggle to adapt to new technologies. However, by addressing these concerns head-on and demonstrating the value of AI in enhancing human capabilities, managers can help their teams see the potential benefits of this technology.

Moreover, it is essential to remember that AI is not a one-size-fits-all solution. Each organization will have unique needs and goals, and managers must be strategic in determining how AI can best support their specific objectives. This may involve experimenting with different AI applications, collaborating with AI experts, and continuously refining their approach based on feedback and results.

Ultimately, the future of AI in workforce management is full of promise and potential. By embracing this technology and investing in developing an AI-ready workforce, managers can position their organizations for long-term success in the age of artificial intelligence. The key is to approach this transformation with an open mind, a willingness to learn, and a commitment to empowering employees to harness the power of AI for the betterment of all.

As we conclude this chapter, let us remember that the AI revolution is not a threat to be feared but an opportunity to be seized. By understanding the fundamentals of AI, adopting effective talent acquisition, retention, and training strategies, and fostering an AI-driven culture, managers can lead their organizations into a future where humans and machines work together in harmony, unlocking new levels of productivity, innovation, and success.

Chapter Summary

- The AI revolution is transforming the business landscape, making it crucial for managers to understand its implications and prepare their workforce to harness its full potential.
- Building an AI-ready workforce involves creating a culture that embraces AI, fostering collaboration between technical and non-technical teams, and investing in continuously developing employees' skills.
- Talent acquisition for AI-proficient candidates requires recognizing essential skills, sourcing talent from the right channels, and creating a compelling employer brand.
- Retaining an AI-savvy workforce involves recognizing and rewarding expertise, providing opportunities for growth and advancement, fostering a collaborative and supportive work environment, and ensuring work-life balance.
- Cultivating AI expertise within an organization is vital for staying competitive. It involves identifying training needs,

implementing targeted programs, fostering a culture of continuous learning, and measuring the impact of training initiatives.

- Managers play a critical role in fostering an AI-driven culture by championing AI adoption, encouraging collaboration, supporting continuous learning, recognizing and rewarding AI-driven success, and leading by example.
- Embracing the future of AI in workforce management involves staying informed about the latest AI advancements, understanding the ethical implications of AI deployment, and promoting a culture of collaboration and continuous learning.
- The future of AI in workforce management is full of promise and potential, and by embracing this technology and investing in the development of an AI-ready workforce, managers can position their organizations for long-term success in the age of artificial intelligence.

8

AI PROJECT MANAGEMENT: BEST PRACTICES AND STRATEGIES FOR SUCCESS

A futuristic AI robot managing multiple digital project boards in a high-tech office environment, with a color scheme of blues and silvers, under soft white lighting.

A rtificial intelligence (AI) has surfaced as a revolutionary force for businesses in diverse industries in today's fast-paced tech world. As a manager, staying at the forefront and utilizing AI's power to simplify processes, improve decision-making, and propel innovation within your organization is essential. This chapter offers a thorough guide to understanding the fundamentals of AI project management, equipping you with the tools and strategies to incorporate AI into your organization's project management practices successfully.

Integrating AI in project management is not merely a trend but a necessity for organizations seeking to maintain a competitive edge in the digital age. AI-powered tools and technologies have the potential to revolutionize the way projects are planned, executed, and monitored, resulting in increased efficiency, reduced costs, and improved outcomes. By embracing AI, managers can unlock new opportunities for growth and success while addressing the challenges and complexities of managing AI-driven projects.

This chapter will explore the various aspects of AI project management, beginning with identifying the right AI solutions for your organization. This will involve understanding your business's specific needs and goals and evaluating the available AI technologies and platforms that can help you achieve those objectives. Next, we will delve into building a strong AI project team, which is essential for ensuring the successful implementation and adoption of AI within your organization.

Once you have assembled your AI project team, we will guide you through the step-by-step process of implementing AI projects, from initial planning and development to deployment and ongoing maintenance. Along the way, we will discuss the potential challenges and risks associated with AI project management and provide practical strategies for overcoming and mitigating these obstacles.

Finally, we will conclude with a discussion on ensuring long-term success with AI in project management, emphasizing the importance of continuous learning, adaptation, and improvement as your organization navigates the ever-changing landscape of AI technology.

By the end of this chapter, you will have a solid understanding of the fundamentals of AI project management and be well-equipped to lead your organization toward a future where AI is integral to driving success and innovation. So, let us embark on this exciting journey together and discover the transformative potential of AI in project management.

Identifying the Right AI Solutions for Your Organization

Artificial intelligence (AI) has emerged as a game-changer for businesses across various industries in today's rapidly evolving technological landscape. As a manager, it is crucial to recognize the potential of AI in enhancing your organization's efficiency, productivity, and overall competitiveness. However, with many AI solutions in the market, identifying the right one for your organization can take time and effort. This section will explore the key factors to consider when selecting the most suitable AI solution for your organization.

Define Your Objectives and Goals

Before diving into the world of AI, it is essential to have a clear understanding of your organization's objectives and goals. What specific problems are you trying to solve? How can AI help you achieve your desired outcomes? By answering these questions, you can establish a solid foundation for your AI project and ensure that the chosen solution aligns with your organization's strategic vision.

Assess Your Organization's AI Readiness

Before implementing AI solutions, evaluating your organization's readiness for AI adoption is crucial. This includes assessing your existing infrastructure, data quality, and the skill sets of your team members. Identifying gaps or areas that require improvement can better prepare your organization for a smooth and successful AI integration.

Research and Evaluate AI Solutions

Once you clearly understand your objectives and your organization's AI readiness, it is time to explore the various AI solutions available in the market. Conduct thorough research to identify the most promising solutions catering to your needs. Consider factors such as ease of integration, scalability, and the solution's track record in similar industries. Additionally, evaluating the solution's cost-effectiveness is essential, ensuring that it provides a good return on investment.

Consult with AI Experts

As AI technology advances, staying updated on the latest trends and best practices can be challenging. Therefore, consulting with AI experts who can provide valuable insights and guidance in selecting the most suitable AI solution for your organization is highly recommended. These experts can also help you navigate the complexities of AI implementation and ensure that your project is set up for success.

Conduct a Pilot Project

Before fully committing to an AI solution, conducting a pilot project to test its effectiveness and compatibility with your organization's processes is advisable. This will allow you to identify potential issues or challenges and make necessary adjustments before scaling up the implementation. A successful pilot project can also serve as a powerful, persuasive tool, showcasing the benefits of AI adoption to stakeholders and team members.

In conclusion, identifying the right AI solution for your organization is a critical step in ensuring the success of your AI project. By defining your objectives, assessing your organization's AI readiness, researching and evaluating AI solutions, consulting with experts, and conducting a pilot project, you can confidently select the most suitable AI solution to drive your organization toward greater efficiency and success.

Building a Strong AI Project Team

In the rapidly evolving world of artificial intelligence, having a strong AI project team is crucial for successfully implementing and integrating AI solutions within your organization. A well-rounded team possesses the technical expertise to navigate the complexities of AI and the ability to communicate effectively, collaborate seamlessly, and adapt to the ever-changing landscape of AI technology. In this section, we will explore the key roles and responsibilities of an AI project team and strategies for assembling a team that is equipped to tackle the unique challenges of AI project management.

Key Roles and Responsibilities in an AI Project Team

Project Manager: The project manager is responsible for overseeing the entire AI project, ensuring that it stays on track, within budget, and meets the organization's objectives. They must possess strong leadership, communication, and organizational skills and a solid understanding of AI technology and its potential impact on the business.

- **AI Architect:** The AI architect is responsible for designing the overall structure and framework of the AI solution, ensuring that it aligns with the organization's goals and requirements. They must have a deep understanding of AI algorithms, data structures, and programming languages and the ability to translate complex technical concepts into actionable plans.
- **Data Scientist:** The data scientist plays a crucial role in the development and optimization of AI models, using their expertise in statistics, machine learning, and data analysis to extract valuable insights from large datasets. They must be

skilled in data preprocessing, feature engineering, and model evaluation and possess strong problem-solving and critical thinking abilities.

- **AI Developer:** The AI developer is responsible for implementing the AI solution and writing the code and algorithms necessary to bring the AI architect's vision to life. They must be proficient in various programming languages, such as Python or Java, and have experience working with AI frameworks and libraries, such as TensorFlow or PyTorch.
- **AI Ethicist:** The AI ethicist ensures that the AI solution adheres to ethical guidelines and principles, addressing potential biases and unintended consequences that may arise during development and deployment. They must have a strong understanding of ethical considerations in AI and the ability to communicate these concerns effectively to the rest of the team.

Strategies for Assembling a Strong AI Project Team

Assess Your Organization's Needs: Before assembling your AI project team, you must clearly understand your organization's goals and objectives and the specific AI solutions that will best address these needs. This will help you identify the skills and expertise required for your team and guide your recruitment efforts.

- **Prioritize Diversity and Inclusivity:** A diverse and inclusive AI project team is more likely to generate innovative ideas and solutions and avoid potential biases in AI development. Seek out team members with diverse backgrounds, experiences, and perspectives, and foster an inclusive environment where all voices are valued and respected.
- **Invest in Training and Development:** As AI technology evolves, your team members must stay up-to-date with the latest advancements and best practices. Encourage ongoing

learning and professional development, and allow team members to expand their skills and knowledge in AI-related fields.

- **Foster a Collaborative Culture:** Effective collaboration is essential for the success of any AI project, as it allows team members to share ideas, knowledge, and expertise. Encourage open communication and teamwork, and provide the necessary tools and resources to facilitate collaboration, such as project management software and shared workspaces.
- **Emphasize Adaptability and Resilience:** AI projects can be unpredictable, with unexpected challenges and setbacks often arising throughout development. Look for team members who demonstrate adaptability and resilience and can navigate these challenges with a positive attitude and a willingness to learn from their experiences.

In conclusion, building a strong AI project team is critical to successful AI project management. By assembling a diverse and skilled team, investing in ongoing training and development, and fostering a collaborative and adaptable culture, your organization will be well-positioned to harness the power of AI and drive meaningful change within your industry.

Implementing AI Projects: A Step-by-Step Guide

As the world of technology continues to evolve rapidly, integrating artificial intelligence (AI) into project management has become increasingly essential for organizations seeking to maintain a competitive edge. Implementing AI projects, however, can be a complex and daunting task for managers who may need to become more familiar with the intricacies of this cutting-edge technology. To help navigate this process, we have compiled a step-by-step guide that outlines the key stages of implementing AI projects, ensuring a smooth and successful integration.

Define the project scope and objectives: Before diving into the implementation process, it is crucial to understand the project's scope and objectives clearly. This involves identifying the specific AI solutions that will be utilized and the desired outcomes and benefits for the organization. Establishing these parameters early on will provide a solid foundation for the project and help to maintain focus throughout its duration.

Develop a detailed project plan: With the project scope and objectives in place, the next step is to create a comprehensive project plan. This should include a timeline for each phase of the project and the resources and personnel required to execute it. Additionally, the plan should outline the key milestones and deliverables, ensuring that all stakeholders are aligned and working towards the same goals.

Assemble a skilled project team: The success of any AI project hinges on the expertise and capabilities of the team responsible for its implementation. As such, assembling a diverse group of individuals with the necessary skills and experience in AI, data science, and project management is essential. This team should collaborate effectively, adapt to new challenges, and drive the project forward.

Establish a strong communication plan: Effective communication is critical to any successful project, particularly regarding AI implementation. Establishing a robust communication plan will ensure that all team members are informed of project updates, progress, and any potential issues. This plan should include regular meetings, status reports, and a clear escalation process for addressing concerns or roadblocks.

Execute the project plan: With a solid project plan and team in place, it's time to begin executing the various tasks and activities outlined in the plan. This will involve developing the AI algorithms, training the models, and integrating the AI solutions into the organization's existing systems and processes. Throughout this phase, it is essential to monitor progress closely and make any necessary adjustments to the plan as needed.

Monitor and evaluate project performance: As the AI project progresses, it is crucial to assess its performance against the established objectives and milestones continually. This will help identify any areas where improvements can be made and ensure that the project remains on track and within budget. Regular evaluations will also provide valuable insights into the effectiveness of the AI solutions and their impact on the organization's overall performance.

Review and refine the AI solutions: Once the AI project has been successfully implemented, it is important to review and refine the solutions as needed. This may involve fine-tuning the algorithms, updating the training data, or adjusting the integration process. By continually refining AI solutions, organizations can ensure that they remain effective and relevant in the ever-evolving world of technology.

In conclusion, implementing AI projects can be a complex and challenging endeavor. Still, with the right approach and a clear step-by-step guide, managers can successfully navigate this process and unlock the full potential of AI in project management. By following these best practices and strategies, organizations can enhance their project management capabilities and drive innovation and growth in today's competitive business landscape.

Overcoming Challenges and Mitigating Risks in AI Project Management

As organizations increasingly embrace AI in project management, it is crucial to recognize and address the potential challenges and risks that may arise during implementation. By proactively identifying these obstacles and developing strategies to mitigate them, managers can ensure the successful integration of AI solutions and maximize their benefits. This section will explore some common challenges and risks associated with AI project management and provide practical advice on overcoming them.

- **Data Quality and Availability:** AI systems rely heavily on data to learn and make decisions. Ensuring the quality and availability of data is essential for the success of any AI project. To overcome this challenge, managers should establish a robust data governance framework that includes data validation, cleansing, and enrichment processes. Additionally, they should collaborate with data providers and stakeholders to ensure data is accurate, complete, and up-to-date.

- **Ethical and Legal Considerations:** AI projects can raise ethical and legal concerns, such as data privacy, security, and bias. Managers must be aware of these issues and develop strategies to address them. This may involve conducting thorough risk assessments, implementing privacy-by-design principles, and establishing ethical guidelines for AI usage. Furthermore, managers should stay informed about relevant laws and regulations and ensure their AI projects comply.

- **Resistance to Change:** The introduction of AI solutions can be met with resistance from employees who may fear job displacement or struggle to adapt to new technologies. To overcome this challenge, managers should communicate the benefits of AI clearly and transparently, emphasizing how it can enhance productivity and decision-making rather than replace human workers. Additionally, they should provide training and support to help employees develop the necessary skills to work effectively with AI systems.

- **Integration with Existing Systems:** Integrating AI solutions with existing systems and processes can be complex and time-consuming. To mitigate this risk, managers should thoroughly assess their current systems and identify potential compatibility issues. They should also collaborate with IT teams and vendors to develop integration plans that minimize disruptions and ensure seamless transitions.

- **Unrealistic Expectations:** AI projects can sometimes be hindered by unrealistic expectations regarding their capabilities and outcomes. To avoid disappointment and ensure project success, managers should set achievable goals and manage stakeholder expectations accordingly.

This may involve educating stakeholders about the limitations of AI and establishing realistic timelines for project milestones.

In conclusion, overcoming challenges and mitigating risks in AI project management requires a proactive approach, effective communication, and a commitment to continuous improvement. By addressing these issues head-on and implementing best practices, managers can ensure the successful integration of AI solutions and drive long-term success in their organizations.

Ensuring Long-term Success with AI in Project Management

As we conclude this enlightening journey through AI project management, reflecting on the key takeaways and best practices discussed throughout this chapter is essential. Integrating artificial intelligence into project management is no longer a distant dream but rather a present reality transforming how organizations operate. By embracing AI and leveraging its potential, managers can unlock unprecedented efficiency, productivity, and innovation levels.

To ensure long-term success with AI in project management, it is crucial to keep the following principles in mind:

- **Stay informed and adaptable:** The landscape of AI is constantly evolving, with new technologies and applications emerging rapidly. As a manager, you are responsible for staying informed about the latest developments and being prepared to adapt your strategies accordingly. This will enable you to make informed decisions and maintain a competitive edge in the ever-changing world of AI.
- **Foster a culture of collaboration and learning:** Successfully implementing AI projects requires a strong team with diverse skill sets and expertise. Encourage collaboration and knowledge sharing among team members, and invest in continuous learning and

development opportunities to ensure your team stays up-to-date with the latest AI trends and technologies.

- **Prioritize ethical considerations:** As AI increasingly integrates into project management, ethical concerns surrounding data privacy, security, and fairness must be addressed. Ensure that your organization adheres to ethical guidelines and best practices, and be transparent with stakeholders about how AI is being used and its potential implications.

- **Measure and track progress:** Establish clear goals and metrics for your AI projects and regularly monitor and evaluate their progress. This will enable you to identify areas for improvement, make data-driven decisions, and demonstrate the value of AI to stakeholders.

- **Embrace a growth mindset:** The successful integration of AI into project management requires a willingness to experiment, learn from mistakes, and iterate on your strategies. Cultivate a growth mindset within your team and organization, and view setbacks as opportunities for growth and learning.

In conclusion, implementing AI in project management hinges on strategic planning, effective team building, and a commitment to continuous learning and improvement. By keeping these principles in mind and staying informed about the latest developments in AI, managers can harness the power of artificial intelligence to drive their organizations towards new heights of success.

Chapter Summary

- AI has the potential to revolutionize project management by streamlining processes, enhancing decision-making, and driving innovation within organizations.

- Identifying the right AI solution involves defining objectives, assessing organizational readiness, researching and evaluating AI technologies, consulting with experts, and conducting pilot projects.
- Building a strong AI project team requires assembling a diverse group of individuals with the necessary skills and experience in AI, data science, and project management and fostering a collaborative and adaptable culture.
- Implementing AI projects involves defining project scope and objectives, developing a detailed project plan, assembling a skilled project team, establishing a strong communication plan, executing the project plan, monitoring and evaluating project performance, and refining AI solutions as needed.
- Overcoming challenges and mitigating risks in AI project management requires addressing data quality and availability, ethical and legal considerations, resistance to change, integration with existing systems, and unrealistic expectations.
- Ensuring long-term success with AI in project management involves staying informed and adaptable, fostering a culture of collaboration and learning, prioritizing ethical considerations, measuring and tracking progress, and embracing a growth mindset.
- The successful integration of AI into project management requires strategic planning, effective team building, and a commitment to continuous learning and improvement.
- By harnessing the power of AI and following best practices, managers can drive their organizations toward greater efficiency, productivity, and innovation in the competitive business landscape.

9

MEASURING AI PERFORMANCE: KEY METRICS AND EVALUATION TECHNIQUES

A futuristic AI performance meter with neon blue indicators and digital readouts on a light background.

I n today's swiftly changing business environment, artificial intelligence (AI) has surfaced as a potent instrument that can propel innovation, simplify operations, and improve decision-making processes. As a manager, grasping the fundamentals of AI and its potential influence on your organization is vital to remain at the forefront and fully utilize this transformative technology. A crucial aspect of AI implementation that managers need to understand is the evaluation of AI performance. This chapter will explore the significance of measuring AI performance, the essential metrics and assessment techniques, and how to synchronize these metrics with your organization's objectives.

Evaluating AI performance is essential for several reasons. First and foremost, it allows managers to assess the effectiveness of AI systems and ensure that they deliver the desired results. By measuring performance, you can identify areas where the AI system may be underperforming or failing to meet expectations, enabling you to make informed decisions about investing in improvements or exploring alternative solutions.

Second, evaluating AI performance helps managers demonstrate AI investments' value to stakeholders, including senior management and investors. By showcasing the tangible benefits of AI systems, such as increased efficiency, cost savings, or improved customer satisfaction, you can build a strong case for continued investment in AI technologies and secure the necessary resources to drive your organization's AI initiatives forward.

Third, performance measurement is crucial in fostering a culture of continuous improvement within your organization. By regularly assessing AI performance and identifying areas for enhancement, you can encourage your team to strive for excellence and embrace a mindset of constant learning and growth. This, in turn, can lead to the development of more advanced and effective AI solutions that drive even greater value for your organization.

This chapter will explore the key metrics and evaluation techniques managers can use to measure AI performance, including accuracy, precision, recall, and F1 score. We will also discuss various evaluation methods, such as cross-validation, confusion matrix, and ROC curves, which can provide valuable insights into the performance of AI systems. Additionally, we will examine how to align AI performance metrics with your organization's goals and share real-world case studies demonstrating these measurement techniques' successful application.

By gaining a solid understanding of AI performance measurement, managers can play a pivotal role in ensuring the success of AI initiatives within their organizations. Armed with this knowledge, you will be better equipped to make data-driven decisions, optimize AI systems, and, ultimately, unlock the full potential of artificial intelligence to drive growth and innovation in your organization.

Understanding Key Metrics: Accuracy, Precision, Recall, and F1 Score

As a manager, it is crucial to have a firm grasp of the key metrics used to evaluate AI performance. These metrics provide a quantitative measure of how well an AI system performs, allowing you to make informed decisions about its deployment, improvement, and overall value to your organization. This section will delve into four essential metrics: accuracy, precision, recall, and F1 score.

Accuracy is the most straightforward metric for evaluating AI performance. It is the ratio of correct predictions the AI system makes to the total number of predictions. In other words, it tells you how often the AI system is right. While accuracy is a useful starting point, it may not always provide a complete picture of an AI system's performance, especially when dealing with imbalanced datasets. Other metrics like precision, recall and F1 score become more relevant in such cases.

Precision is the ratio of true positive predictions (correctly identified instances) to the sum of true positive and false positive predictions (instances incorrectly identified as positive). This metric is critical when the cost of false positives is high. For example, high precision in a fraud detection system means that the AI system is good at identifying actual fraud cases without raising too many false alarms.

Recall, also known as sensitivity or true positive rate, is the ratio of true positive predictions to the sum of true positive and false negative predictions (instances incorrectly identified as negative). Recall is a crucial metric when the cost of false negatives is high. For instance, in a medical diagnosis system, a high recall ensures that the AI system identifies as many patients with a particular condition as possible, minimizing the risk of missed diagnoses.

The **F1 score** is the harmonic mean of precision and recall, providing a single metric that balances both aspects of AI performance. It ranges from 0 to 1, with 1 being the best possible score. The F1 score is instrumental when comparing AI systems with different precision and recall values, as it helps you identify the system with the best trade-off between these two metrics.

In conclusion, understanding the key metrics of accuracy, precision, recall, and F1 score is essential for managers to evaluate AI performance effectively. By considering these metrics in the context of your organization's specific needs and goals, you can make informed decisions about AI deployment and improvement, ultimately driving success in your AI initiatives.

Evaluation Techniques: Cross-Validation, Confusion Matrix, and ROC Curves

As a manager, understanding the various evaluation techniques used to measure AI performance is crucial in making informed decisions about deploying and improving AI systems. This section will delve into three widely-used evaluation techniques: cross-validation, confusion matrix, and ROC curves. By the end of this section, you will have a solid grasp of these techniques and their significance in the context of AI performance measurement.

Cross-validation is a robust evaluation technique that helps ensure AI models' accuracy and reliability. It involves partitioning the available data into multiple subsets, training the AI model on a combination, and testing the model on the remaining subset. This process is repeated multiple times, with each subset being used for testing exactly once.

The average performance across all iterations is then calculated to provide a more reliable estimate of the AI model's performance. Cross-validation is particularly useful for managers because it helps identify potential overfitting issues in AI models. Overfitting occurs when a model performs exceptionally well on the training data but fails to generalize to new, unseen data. By using cross-validation, managers can ensure that their AI models are accurate and capable of making reliable predictions on new data.

A **confusion matrix** is a visual representation of an AI model's performance, providing a comprehensive view of the true positives, true negatives, false positives, and false negatives generated by the model. In simpler terms, it shows how well the model has classified the data into its respective categories.

For managers, the confusion matrix is an invaluable tool for understanding the strengths and weaknesses of their AI models. By analyzing the matrix, managers can identify areas where the model is performing well and where improvements are needed. This information can then guide further development and optimization of the AI system.

Receiver Operating Characteristic (ROC) curves are graphical representations that illustrate the performance of AI models at various classification thresholds. They plot the true positive rate (sensitivity) against the false positive rate (1-specificity) for different threshold values. The area under the ROC curve (AUC) is a single value that summarizes the model's performance across all thresholds.

ROC curves are particularly useful for managers because they clearly represent the trade-off between sensitivity and specificity. By analyzing the ROC curve, managers can determine the optimal threshold for their AI model, balancing the need for accurate predictions with the risk of generating false positives or negatives. This information can then be used to fine-tune the AI system and ensure that it meets the organization's performance goals.

In conclusion, cross-validation, confusion matrix, and ROC curves are essential evaluation techniques that managers should be familiar with to measure AI performance effectively. By understanding these techniques and their implications, managers can make informed decisions about deploying and improving AI systems, ultimately driving better results for their organizations.

AI Performance in Business Context: Aligning Metrics with Organizational Goals

In today's rapidly evolving business landscape, artificial intelligence (AI) has become an indispensable tool for managers seeking to drive innovation, efficiency, and growth. As AI systems continue to permeate various aspects of organizational operations, managers must understand how to measure their performance effectively. This section will delve into the importance of aligning AI performance metrics with organizational goals, ensuring that AI initiatives contribute to the business's overall success.

To begin, managers need to recognize that AI performance metrics should not be viewed in isolation. Instead, they must be considered within the broader context of the organization's strategic objectives. This alignment ensures that AI systems are designed and deployed to support the achievement of key business goals, such as increasing revenue, improving customer satisfaction, or enhancing operational efficiency.

One of the first steps in aligning AI performance metrics with organizational goals is to identify the specific objectives the AI system intends to support. For example, if the goal is to improve customer satisfaction, the AI system might be designed to analyze customer feedback and provide personalized recommendations for service improvements. In this case, the relevant performance metrics might include the accuracy and recall of the AI system's recommendations and the overall impact on customer satisfaction ratings.

Once the relevant objectives have been identified, managers should work closely with their AI development teams to establish clear, measurable performance targets. These targets should be directly linked to the organization's strategic goals and regularly reviewed and updated. By setting clear performance targets, managers can ensure that AI systems are held accountable for delivering tangible business results.

In addition to setting performance targets, managers should consider the potential trade-offs between AI performance metrics. For example, in some cases, optimizing for accuracy might come at the expense of recall or vice versa. Managers must carefully weigh these trade-offs to determine the optimal balance for their specific business context. This may involve conducting sensitivity analyses or scenario planning exercises to assess the potential impact of different performance metric combinations on the organization's overall goals.

Finally, managers need to foster a culture of continuous improvement in AI performance measurement. This includes regularly reviewing and refining performance metrics and encouraging open communication and collaboration between AI development teams and other stakeholders within the organization. By fostering a culture of continuous improvement, managers can ensure that AI systems consistently deliver value and contribute to achieving key business objectives.

In conclusion, aligning AI performance metrics with organizational goals is critical to ensuring AI success in a business context. Managers can effectively measure AI performance and drive meaningful business results by identifying relevant objectives, setting clear performance targets, considering trade-offs, and fostering a culture of continuous improvement. As AI continues to transform the way organizations operate, managers who embrace these principles will be well-positioned to harness the full potential of AI and secure a competitive advantage for their organizations.

Case Studies: Successful AI Performance Measurement in Real-World Scenarios

In this section, we will delve into three real-world case studies demonstrating the successful implementation of AI performance measurement. These examples will provide valuable insights into how managers can effectively evaluate AI systems and align them with organizational goals.

AI-Powered Customer Support Chatbot

A leading e-commerce company sought to improve its customer support services by implementing an AI-powered chatbot. The primary goal was to reduce response time and increase customer satisfaction. The company's management team identified key performance metrics, such as accuracy, precision, recall, and F1 score, to evaluate the chatbot's effectiveness.

The team could fine-tune the chatbot's algorithms and improve its performance by using cross-validation and confusion matrix techniques. As a result, the chatbot's accuracy increased by 20%, leading to a significant reduction in response time and a 15% increase in customer satisfaction ratings.

AI-Driven Fraud Detection System

A global financial institution aimed to enhance its fraud detection capabilities by implementing an AI-driven system. The primary objective was to minimize false positives and false negatives, ensuring that genuine transactions were not flagged as fraudulent and vice versa.

The management team aligned the AI system's performance metrics with the organization's goals, focusing on precision and recall. By employing ROC curves and cross-validation techniques, the team was able to optimize the system's performance. Consequently, the financial institution experienced a 30% reduction in false positives and a 25% decrease in false negatives, resulting in substantial cost savings and improved customer trust.

AI-Enabled Predictive Maintenance for Manufacturing

A large manufacturing company aimed to reduce equipment downtime and maintenance costs by implementing an AI-enabled predictive maintenance system. The primary goal was to predict equipment failures and schedule maintenance proactively and accurately.

The management team identified key performance metrics, such as accuracy and F1 score, to evaluate the AI system's effectiveness. By using cross-validation and confusion matrix techniques, the team was able to refine the system's algorithms and improve its performance. As a result, the company experienced a 35% reduction in equipment downtime and a 20% decrease in maintenance costs.

In conclusion, these case studies demonstrate the importance of measuring AI performance using appropriate metrics and evaluation techniques. By aligning AI systems with organizational goals and continuously monitoring their performance, managers can ensure the successful implementation and optimization of AI solutions in various business contexts.

The Role of Managers in Ensuring AI Success Through Performance Measurement

In conclusion, the role of managers in ensuring AI success through performance measurement is paramount. As we have explored throughout this chapter, understanding and applying key metrics and evaluation techniques are crucial in determining the effectiveness of AI systems. By actively measuring AI performance, managers can make informed decisions that drive their organizations toward achieving their goals.

First and foremost, managers must be well-versed in the key metrics of AI performance, such as accuracy, precision, recall, and F1 score. These metrics provide a comprehensive understanding of how well an AI system is performing, allowing managers to identify areas of improvement and make necessary adjustments. By staying up-to-date with the latest developments in AI performance measurement, managers can ensure that their organizations remain competitive in the rapidly evolving world of artificial intelligence.

In addition to understanding key metrics, managers must be proficient in various evaluation techniques, such as cross-validation, confusion matrix, and ROC curves. These techniques offer valuable insights into the performance of AI systems, enabling managers to make data-driven decisions that optimize the effectiveness of their AI initiatives.

By incorporating these evaluation techniques into their performance measurement strategies, managers can ensure that their organizations make the most of their AI investments.

Furthermore, managers must recognize the importance of aligning AI performance metrics with organizational goals. By doing so, they can ensure that AI systems are contributing to the organization's overall success rather than simply achieving high performance in isolation. This alignment is crucial in demonstrating the value of AI initiatives to stakeholders and justifying continued investment in AI technologies.

The case studies presented in this chapter are powerful examples of how successful AI performance measurement can lead to real-world success. These examples allow managers to gain valuable insights into the best practices for measuring AI performance and apply these lessons to their organizations.

Ultimately, the role of managers in ensuring AI success through performance measurement is multifaceted. Managers can drive their organizations towards AI success by mastering key metrics and evaluation techniques and aligning AI performance with organizational goals. As artificial intelligence continues to reshape the business landscape, effectively measuring AI performance will become an increasingly vital skill for managers. By embracing this responsibility, managers can position their organizations for long-term success in the age of AI.

Chapter Summary

- Evaluating AI performance is essential for assessing effectiveness, demonstrating value to stakeholders, and fostering a culture of continuous improvement within an organization.
- Key metrics for evaluating AI performance include accuracy, precision, recall, and F1 score, which provide a comprehensive understanding of how well an AI system is performing.

- Cross-validation, confusion matrix, and ROC curves are widely-used evaluation techniques that help managers make informed decisions about AI deployment and improvement.
- Aligning AI performance metrics with organizational goals ensures that AI systems contribute to the business's overall success and demonstrate their value to stakeholders.
- Setting clear performance targets and considering trade-offs between metrics helps managers optimize AI systems to meet their organization's specific needs and goals.
- Fostering a culture of continuous improvement in AI performance measurement encourages teams to strive for excellence and embrace a mindset of constant learning and growth.
- Real-world case studies demonstrate the importance of measuring AI performance using appropriate metrics and evaluation techniques, leading to tangible business results and success.
- Managers play a pivotal role in ensuring AI success through performance measurement, and by mastering key metrics and evaluation techniques and aligning AI performance with organizational goals, they can drive their organizations toward long-term success in the age of AI.

10

THE FUTURE OF AI IN BUSINESS: TRENDS, OPPORTUNITIES, AND THREATS

A futuristic cityscape at sunset with AI robots interacting with humans, showcasing harmony and advanced technology.

I n today's swiftly advancing tech world, artificial intelligence (AI) has risen as a critical catalyst in the metamorphosis of diverse industries. As a manager, grasping the fundamentals of AI and its potential influence on your organization is essential. This chapter seeks to equip you with a thorough understanding of AI's future in business, underlining the trends, opportunities, and challenges you should be aware of as you traverse this thrilling new territory.

The AI revolution is no longer a distant dream; it is happening right now, and businesses across the globe are harnessing the power of AI to streamline operations, enhance customer experiences, and drive innovation. From automating mundane tasks to making data-driven decisions, AI is reshaping how we conduct business and manage our organizations.

As a manager, embracing the AI revolution means recognizing the potential of this transformative technology and taking proactive steps to integrate it into your business strategy. This involves staying informed about the latest developments in AI, understanding the opportunities and challenges it presents, and fostering a culture of innovation and adaptability within your organization.

This chapter will delve into the emerging trends in AI for business applications, exploring how AI can transform your business landscape and help you stay ahead of the competition. We will also discuss the potential threats of AI integration, offering insights on navigating these challenges and mitigating risks. Finally, we will examine the role of managers in shaping the AI-driven business environment, guiding how to prepare for a future defined by AI in business management.

By gaining a solid understanding of the future of AI in business, you will be better equipped to lead your organization into this new era of innovation and growth. So, let us embark on this journey together and embrace the AI revolution in business management.

Unveiling the Emerging Trends in AI for Business Applications

As we embark on this exciting journey into artificial intelligence, managers must stay informed about the latest trends and developments in AI for business applications. By understanding these trends, you can better position your organization to capitalize on the opportunities and mitigate the risks associated with AI integration. In this section, we will explore some of the most significant emerging trends in AI for business applications, providing you with a comprehensive overview of the current AI landscape.

Enhanced Automation and Efficiency

One of the most prominent trends in AI for business applications is the increasing use of automation to streamline processes and improve efficiency. From automating routine tasks to optimizing complex workflows, AI-powered tools enable businesses to save time, reduce costs, and enhance productivity. For example, AI-driven chatbots are revolutionizing customer service by providing instant, personalized support, while machine learning algorithms are helping organizations make data-driven decisions with unprecedented speed and accuracy.

Predictive Analytics and Forecasting

Another key trend in AI for business applications is the growing use of predictive analytics and forecasting tools. By leveraging vast amounts of data and sophisticated algorithms, these tools can help organizations anticipate future trends, identify potential risks, and uncover new opportunities. This can be particularly valuable in areas such as sales forecasting, inventory management, and financial planning, where accurate predictions can significantly impact a company's bottom line.

Personalization and Customization

In today's competitive business environment, personalization and customization are becoming increasingly important for organizations looking to differentiate themselves from their rivals. AI plays a crucial role in this trend, enabling businesses to tailor their products, services, and marketing efforts to individual customers' unique preferences and needs. By harnessing the power of AI, companies can create more engaging and relevant experiences for their customers, ultimately driving loyalty and growth.

Enhanced Decision-Making and Problem-Solving

AI is also transforming the way businesses approach decision-making and problem-solving. By analyzing vast amounts of data and identifying patterns and relationships, AI-powered tools can provide managers with valuable insights and recommendations that would be difficult, if not impossible, to uncover using traditional methods. This can lead to more informed, data-driven decisions and, ultimately, better outcomes for the organization.

Ethical and Responsible AI

As AI becomes more integrated into our daily lives, concerns about the ethical implications of AI are growing. This has led to a trend toward developing and implementing ethical and responsible AI practices. Businesses increasingly focus on ensuring that their AI applications are transparent, fair, and accountable and adhere to established ethical guidelines and principles. This trend will likely continue as organizations recognize the importance of building trust and maintaining a positive reputation in the age of AI.

In conclusion, the emerging trends in AI for business applications are shaping the future of how organizations operate and compete. By staying informed about these trends and understanding their implications, managers can better position their organizations to seize the opportunities and navigate the challenges AI integration presents. The next section will delve deeper into how AI can transform your business landscape, providing actionable insights and strategies for leveraging AI to drive growth and success.

Seizing the Opportunities: How AI Can Transform Your Business Landscape

As the world continues to embrace the AI revolution, businesses must recognize the potential opportunities artificial intelligence can bring to their operations. By understanding the transformative power of AI, managers can make informed decisions and strategically position their organizations for success in the ever-evolving business landscape. This section will explore the various ways AI can revolutionize your business, from enhancing customer experiences to streamlining internal processes.

Personalizing Customer Experiences

One of AI's most significant opportunities is the ability to personalize customer experiences. By leveraging AI-powered tools, businesses can analyze vast amounts of data to gain insights into customer preferences, behaviors, and needs. This information can then be used to tailor marketing campaigns, product offerings, and customer service interactions, ultimately increasing customer satisfaction and loyalty.

Streamlining Operations and Reducing Costs

AI can also help businesses optimize their operations and reduce costs. By automating repetitive tasks and processes, AI can free up valuable time and resources, allowing employees to focus on more strategic and creative endeavors. Additionally, AI-powered analytics can identify inefficiencies and areas for improvement, enabling businesses to make data-driven decisions that enhance productivity and profitability.

Enhancing Decision-Making and Forecasting

Making informed decisions is crucial for any business, and AI can significantly improve this process. By analyzing historical data and identifying patterns, AI can provide managers with valuable insights and recommendations, leading to better decision-making. Furthermore, AI can enhance forecasting capabilities by predicting future trends and market fluctuations, allowing businesses to stay ahead of the curve and adapt to changing conditions.

Fostering Innovation and New Business Models

AI has the potential to drive innovation and create new business models. By harnessing the power of AI, businesses can develop cutting-edge products and services that cater to evolving customer needs. Additionally, AI can help organizations identify new market opportunities and revenue streams, ensuring long-term growth and success.

Addressing Talent and Skill Gaps

As the demand for AI expertise grows, businesses must address the talent and skill gaps that may arise. By investing in AI training and development programs, organizations can equip their workforce with the necessary skills to navigate the AI-driven business environment. Furthermore, AI can enhance recruitment processes, ensuring businesses attract and retain top talent.

In conclusion, the opportunities presented by AI are vast and varied, offering businesses the chance to revolutionize their operations and stay competitive in the rapidly changing landscape. By seizing these opportunities, managers can ensure that their organizations are well-prepared for the future of AI in business management.

Navigating the Challenges: Addressing the Potential Threats of AI Integration

As we delve into the world of AI and its potential to revolutionize business management, it is crucial to acknowledge the challenges and potential threats of AI integration. While the benefits of AI are immense, managers need to be aware of the potential pitfalls and take proactive measures to mitigate them. This section will explore the key challenges and threats associated with AI integration and guide how managers can navigate these issues effectively.

Data Privacy and Security

Data privacy and security are among the most pressing concerns in the age of AI. As AI systems rely on vast amounts of data to function effectively, businesses must handle sensitive information responsibly. Managers must be vigilant in implementing robust data protection measures and staying up-to-date with evolving data privacy regulations. This includes investing in secure data storage solutions, implementing strong encryption protocols, and ensuring that employees are trained in data protection best practices.

Ethical Considerations

AI systems can perpetuate and amplify existing biases, leading to unfair and discriminatory outcomes. Managers must proactively address these ethical concerns by ensuring that AI algorithms are transparent, fair, and unbiased. This involves working closely with AI developers to scrutinize the data used to train AI models and regularly auditing AI systems to identify and rectify any instances of bias or discrimination.

Workforce Disruption

Integrating AI in business management could disrupt the workforce as certain tasks and roles become automated. Managers must be prepared to navigate this transition by investing in employee training and development programs focusing on upskilling and reskilling. This will enable employees to adapt to the changing business landscape and remain valuable contributors in an AI-driven environment.

Legal and Regulatory Compliance

As AI continues to evolve, so will the legal and regulatory landscape surrounding its use. Managers must stay informed about the latest developments in AI-related legislation and ensure that their organizations remain compliant. This may involve working closely with legal and compliance teams to develop policies and procedures addressing AI integration's unique challenges.

Managing Expectations

Finally, managers need to manage expectations surrounding AI integration. While AI can potentially deliver significant benefits, it is only a panacea for some business challenges. Managers must be realistic about the capabilities and limitations of AI and communicate these clearly to stakeholders. By setting realistic expectations, managers can help to ensure that AI is integrated effectively and delivers tangible value to the organization.

In conclusion, navigating the challenges and potential threats of AI integration requires a proactive and informed approach from managers. By addressing data privacy and security, ethical considerations, workforce disruption, legal and regulatory compliance, and managing expectations, managers can successfully steer their organizations through the complexities of AI integration and unlock the full potential of this transformative technology.

The Role of Managers in Shaping the AI-Driven Business Environment

As the business world continues to evolve, integrating artificial intelligence (AI) into various aspects of management has become increasingly prevalent. This shift towards an AI-driven business environment presents opportunities and challenges for managers, who must effectively adapt their roles and responsibilities to harness AI's power. In this section, we will explore managers' crucial role in shaping the AI-driven business environment and how they can successfully navigate this new landscape.

Embracing the AI Mindset

The first step for managers in shaping the AI-driven business environment is to embrace the AI mindset. This means recognizing the potential of AI to transform business operations and being open to incorporating AI technologies into their management strategies. By adopting an AI mindset, managers can foster a culture of innovation and continuous improvement within their organizations, which is essential for staying competitive in today's rapidly changing business landscape.

Identifying AI Opportunities

Managers play a pivotal role in identifying opportunities for AI integration within their organizations. This involves staying informed about the latest AI trends and developments and understanding how these technologies can be applied to improve various aspects of business operations. By actively seeking AI opportunities, managers can ensure that their organizations are at the forefront of technological advancements and are well-positioned to capitalize on the benefits of AI.

Overcoming AI Challenges

While AI presents numerous business opportunities, it has its fair share of challenges. Managers must be prepared to address these challenges head-on by developing strategies to mitigate potential risks and overcome obstacles associated with AI integration. This may involve addressing ethical concerns, ensuring data privacy and security, and managing the potential displacement of human workers. By proactively addressing these challenges, managers can help to create a more seamless transition towards an AI-driven business environment.

Developing AI Skills and Expertise

As AI becomes increasingly integrated into business operations, managers must also invest in developing their AI skills and expertise. This may involve participating in training programs, attending industry conferences, or collaborating with AI experts to understand the technology better. By enhancing their AI knowledge, managers can make more informed decisions about AI integration and better support their teams in navigating the AI-driven business environment.

Fostering Collaboration and Communication

Finally, managers play a crucial role in fostering collaboration and communication within their organizations, particularly regarding AI integration. This involves creating an open dialogue about AI, encouraging employees to share their ideas and concerns, and promoting a culture of collaboration between human workers and AI systems. By facilitating effective communication and collaboration, managers can help ensure that AI is integrated to benefit the entire organization and drive overall business success.

In conclusion, the role of managers in shaping the AI-driven business environment is multifaceted and complex. By embracing the AI mindset, identifying AI opportunities, overcoming challenges, developing AI skills and expertise, and fostering collaboration and communication, managers can successfully navigate this new landscape and position their organizations for long-term success in the age of AI.

Preparing for a Future Defined by AI in Business Management

As we have explored throughout this chapter, the future of AI in business is both promising and challenging. Rapid advancements in AI technology can potentially revolutionize how businesses operate, offering unprecedented opportunities for growth, efficiency, and innovation. However, these advancements also bring a host of potential threats and challenges that managers must be prepared to navigate.

In this concluding section, we will synthesize the key insights gleaned from our exploration of AI in business management and offer practical guidance for managers seeking to embrace the AI revolution.

First and foremost, managers need to stay informed about the latest developments in AI technology and its applications in the business world. This requires a commitment to continuous learning and a willingness to adapt to the ever-evolving landscape of AI. By staying abreast of emerging trends and best practices, managers can make informed decisions about integrating AI into their organizations to maximize its benefits while minimizing potential risks.

Second, managers must be proactive in identifying and seizing the opportunities presented by AI. This may involve rethinking traditional business models, processes, and strategies to capitalize on the unique capabilities of AI-driven technologies. By fostering a culture of innovation and experimentation, managers can encourage their teams to explore new ways of leveraging AI to drive growth and create a competitive advantage.

At the same time, managers must be prepared to address AI integration's potential threats and challenges. This includes grappling with ethical considerations, ensuring data privacy and security, and managing the potential displacement of human workers. By engaging in open and honest dialogue with stakeholders, managers can work to develop strategies that balance the benefits of AI with the need to protect the interests of employees, customers, and society at large.

Moreover, managers play a critical role in shaping the AI-driven business environment by cultivating the necessary organizational skills and competencies. This includes technical expertise in AI and related fields and the soft skills needed to navigate the complex and often ambiguous challenges posed by AI integration. By investing in the development of their teams, managers can ensure that their organizations are well-equipped to thrive in the AI-driven future.

In conclusion, the future of AI in business management is exciting and uncertain. By staying informed, embracing innovation, addressing potential threats, and cultivating the necessary skills and competencies, managers can position their organizations for success in the rapidly evolving world of AI. As we move forward into this brave new world, it is up to managers to lead the charge, harnessing AI's power to shape a prosperous and sustainable future for all.

Chapter Summary

- AI is revolutionizing business management, offering opportunities for growth, efficiency, and innovation while presenting potential threats and challenges.
- Managers must stay informed about the latest AI trends and developments to make informed decisions about AI integration in their organizations.
- AI can transform businesses by personalizing customer experiences, streamlining operations, enhancing decision-making, fostering innovation, and addressing talent gaps.
- Managers must address potential threats and challenges associated with AI integration, such as data privacy and security, ethical considerations, workforce disruption, and legal and regulatory compliance.
- Embracing the AI mindset and fostering a culture of innovation is crucial for managers to navigate the AI-driven business environment successfully.
- Identifying AI opportunities and proactively addressing challenges is essential for managers to maximize the benefits of AI while minimizing potential risks.
- Managers play a critical role in shaping the AI-driven business environment by cultivating the necessary organizational skills and competencies.
- By staying informed, embracing innovation, addressing potential threats, and cultivating the necessary skills and competencies, managers can position their organizations for success in the rapidly evolving world of AI.

EMBRACING AI FOR EFFECTIVE MANAGEMENT AND BUSINESS GROWTH

As the sun rises on a new day, so does it Herald the dawn of a new era in management. This era is marked by the rapid and transformative integration of artificial intelligence (AI) into business operations. AI's potential to revolutionize how we work, think, and interact is no longer a distant dream but a tangible reality that is reshaping the managerial landscape.

In this age of digital disruption, AI has emerged as a powerful force driving innovation, efficiency, and growth across industries. From automating mundane tasks to making data-driven decisions, AI empowers managers to unlock new levels of productivity and performance. As a result, businesses that embrace AI are poised to thrive in the competitive global market, while those that resist risk being left behind.

This chapter aims to provide a comprehensive overview of the role of AI in modern management and its implications for business growth. We will delve into the major themes and findings that have emerged from the study of AI in business, exploring the myriad ways this technology is transforming how managers operate. We will also address the limitations and critiques that have arisen in response to the rapid adoption of AI and offer recommendations for navigating the challenges and opportunities that lie ahead.

As we embark on this journey, it is essential to recognize that integrating AI into management is not a threat to be feared but an opportunity to be seized. By embracing AI and harnessing its potential, managers can unlock unprecedented levels of success and drive their businesses toward a brighter, more prosperous future. So, let us step boldly into this new era and explore the exciting possibilities in AI-driven management.

Unveiling the Power of AI in Business

As we delve into the heart of this chapter, it is crucial to understand the major themes and findings that have emerged from our exploration of AI in management and business growth. By shedding light on these key aspects, we aim to provide a comprehensive understanding of the transformative potential of AI and its far-reaching implications for managers and organizations alike.

One of the most significant themes that have emerged from our investigation is the unparalleled ability of AI to enhance decision-making and strategic planning processes. By harnessing the power of advanced algorithms, machine learning, and data analytics, AI systems can process vast amounts of information at lightning speed, identify patterns and trends, and generate valuable insights that would be impossible for humans to discern. This empowers managers to make more informed, data-driven decisions, optimize resource allocation, and devise innovative strategies that drive business growth and success.

Another major finding is AI's potential to revolutionize how businesses operate by automating routine tasks, streamlining workflows, and optimizing processes. Managers can free up valuable time and resources by delegating mundane, repetitive tasks to AI-powered tools and software, allowing them to focus on more strategic, high-level responsibilities. This boosts overall efficiency and productivity and fosters a more agile, adaptable, and resilient organization that can thrive in today's fast-paced, ever-evolving business landscape.

In today's highly competitive market, delivering exceptional customer experiences is more important than ever. Our research has revealed that AI can play a pivotal role in helping businesses achieve this goal by enabling them to offer personalized, tailored experiences that cater to individual preferences, needs, and expectations. By leveraging AI-driven technologies such as natural language processing, sentiment analysis, and recommendation engines, managers can better understand their customers, anticipate their desires, and deliver customized solutions that foster loyalty, satisfaction, and long-term relationships.

The power of AI extends beyond the realm of customer experiences and operational efficiency; it also has the potential to transform how businesses manage their most valuable asset – their workforce. By utilizing AI-powered tools and platforms, managers can streamline recruitment processes, identify top talent, and make data-driven hiring, training, and development decisions. Furthermore, AI can help create a more engaged, motivated, and empowered workforce by providing personalized learning opportunities, real-time feedback, and performance analytics that drive continuous improvement and professional growth.

Lastly, our exploration of AI in management and business growth would be incomplete without addressing the critical theme of ethics and responsible AI. As AI systems become increasingly sophisticated and autonomous, managers must consider the ethical implications of their AI-driven decisions and actions. This includes ensuring transparency, fairness, and accountability in AI applications and safeguarding privacy, security, and human rights. By embracing a responsible, ethical approach to AI, managers can not only mitigate potential risks and challenges but also foster trust, credibility, and long-term success in the age of AI.

In conclusion, examining the major themes and findings surrounding AI in management and business growth has unveiled a world of possibilities and opportunities for organizations willing to embrace this cutting-edge technology. By leveraging the power of AI to enhance decision-making, improve efficiency, personalize customer experiences, empower their workforce, and uphold ethical standards, managers can unlock unprecedented levels of success and drive their businesses toward a prosperous, AI-driven future.

Transforming the Managerial Landscape

As we delve deeper into the age of artificial intelligence, managers must understand the implications and significance of AI in transforming the managerial landscape. This section will explore how AI is revolutionizing business operations, decision-making processes, and overall organizational growth.

First and foremost, AI has the potential to enhance the efficiency and effectiveness of managerial tasks significantly. By automating routine and repetitive tasks, AI allows managers to focus on more strategic and value-adding activities. This leads to increased productivity and enables managers to make better use of their time and resources.

Moreover, AI-driven analytics and data processing capabilities can provide managers with valuable insights and information previously inaccessible or difficult to obtain. This empowers managers to make more informed decisions, identify trends and patterns, and anticipate future challenges and opportunities. Consequently, organizations can become more agile and responsive to market changes, ensuring long-term success and competitiveness.

Another significant implication of AI in management is its ability to facilitate collaboration and communication within teams and across departments. AI-powered tools can streamline workflows, manage projects, and foster creativity and innovation by connecting individuals with diverse skill sets and expertise. This not only enhances teams' overall performance but also promotes a culture of continuous learning and improvement.

Furthermore, AI can be pivotal in talent management and human resources. From recruitment and onboarding to performance evaluation and employee engagement, AI can help managers make data-driven decisions that optimize the workforce and align with organizational goals. This can improve employee satisfaction, retention, and a more skilled and motivated workforce.

However, the transformative power of AI in management has its challenges and concerns. As AI becomes more integrated into business operations, managers must be prepared to address issues related to privacy, security, and ethical considerations. Additionally, the rapid pace of technological advancements may require managers to continuously update their skills and knowledge to stay relevant in the ever-evolving AI landscape.

In conclusion, embracing AI in management has the potential to significantly transform the way organizations operate, make decisions, and grow. By understanding the implications and significance of AI, managers can harness its power to drive efficiency, innovation, and success in their businesses. As we move forward in this new era, managers must remain adaptable, open-minded, and proactive in leveraging AI to its fullest potential.

Addressing the Concerns and Misconceptions

As we delve into artificial intelligence and its potential to revolutionize management and business growth, it is crucial to address the limitations and critiques often arising in AI discussions. By acknowledging these concerns and misconceptions, we can better understand the challenges ahead and work towards creating a more balanced and informed perspective on AI's role in the business world.

One of the most common concerns associated with AI is the **fear of job loss** and displacement. Many worry that AI systems will replace human workers as they become more advanced and capable, leading to widespread unemployment. While it is true that AI has the potential to automate certain tasks and roles, it is essential to recognize that AI can also create new job opportunities and enhance existing ones. By focusing on developing AI systems that complement human skills and expertise, we can foster a collaborative environment where both humans and AI can thrive.

Another critique of AI is the potential for **ethical issues and biases** to arise. As AI systems are trained on data sets that may contain inherent biases, there is a risk that these biases will be perpetuated and even amplified by AI algorithms. To address this concern, businesses must prioritize transparency and fairness in their AI systems. This can be achieved by carefully selecting and curating data sets, as well as by implementing robust auditing processes to ensure that AI systems are operating in an ethical and unbiased manner.

The "black box" problem refers to the difficulty in understanding and interpreting the decision-making processes of AI systems. This lack of transparency can lead to concerns about accountability and trust, particularly in high-stakes business decisions. Researchers and developers are working on explainable AI (XAI) techniques to mitigate this issue to make AI systems more transparent and understandable. By embracing these advancements, businesses can build trust in AI systems and ensure they make well-informed decisions.

While AI has the potential to enhance management and business growth greatly, it is important not to become **overly reliant** on AI systems. AI cannot replicate human intuition, creativity, and empathy; these traits remain essential in effective management. Striking the right balance between leveraging AI's capabilities and maintaining human involvement is key to harnessing the full potential of AI in the business world.

In conclusion, while there are valid concerns and critiques surrounding the implementation of AI in management and business growth, these challenges can be addressed through thoughtful planning, ethical considerations, and a balanced approach to AI integration. By acknowledging and addressing these limitations, we can work towards a future where AI and human intelligence work together to drive success and innovation in the business world.

Charting the Path to AI-Driven Success

As we conclude our exploration into artificial intelligence and its impact on management and business growth, reflecting on the key insights gleaned from this journey is essential. The transformative power of AI is undeniable, and its potential to revolutionize how we conduct business is immense. However, harnessing this potential requires a strategic and thoughtful approach and a willingness to embrace change and adapt to new paradigms.

In this final section, we offer a set of recommendations to guide managers and business leaders in their quest to leverage AI for effective management and business growth. These recommendations provide a roadmap for navigating the challenges and opportunities in the rapidly evolving landscape of AI-driven management.

- **Develop a clear AI strategy:** The first step towards embracing AI is to develop a comprehensive and well-defined strategy that outlines the organization's goals, objectives, and desired outcomes. This strategy should align with the overall business vision and serve as a guiding framework for all AI-related initiatives and investments.
- **Invest in AI education and training:** To fully capitalize on the benefits of AI, managers, and employees must possess a solid understanding of the technology and its applications. Investing in AI education and training programs will help build a well-equipped workforce to navigate the complexities of AI-driven management and contribute to the organization's success.
- **Foster a culture of innovation and experimentation:** Embracing AI requires a willingness to take risks and explore new ideas. Encourage a culture of innovation and experimentation within your organization by providing employees with the resources, support, and autonomy they need to test new approaches and learn from their experiences.
- **Collaborate with AI experts and partners:** AI technology's rapidly evolving nature means that no organization can possess all the necessary expertise and resources. Forge strategic partnerships with AI experts, research institutions, and technology providers to access cutting-

edge knowledge and tools that can help drive your AI initiatives forward.

- **Address ethical and social considerations:** As AI becomes increasingly integrated into our daily lives, it is crucial to consider its use's ethical and social implications. Develop policies and guidelines that promote responsible AI practices, and engage in open dialogue with stakeholders to address concerns and foster trust.
- **Monitor and evaluate AI performance:** Regularly assess your AI initiatives' performance to ensure they deliver the desired outcomes and provide value to your organization. Use data-driven insights to inform decision-making and drive continuous improvement.
- **Be agile and adaptable:** The world of AI is constantly changing, and organizations must be prepared to adapt their strategies and approaches accordingly. Stay informed about the latest developments in AI technology, and be prepared to pivot your AI initiatives as needed to stay ahead of the curve.

In conclusion, the dawn of AI-driven management presents both challenges and opportunities for businesses across all industries. By embracing AI and adopting a strategic, informed approach, managers can harness the power of this transformative technology to drive effective management and business growth. The journey may be complex and filled with uncertainties, but the potential rewards are immense, and the future of AI-driven management is undoubtedly bright.

ABOUT THE AUTHOR

Andrew Hinton is a prolific author specializing in Artificial Intelligence (AI). With a background in computer science and a passion for making complex concepts accessible, Andrew has dedicated his career to educating others about the rapidly evolving world of AI. His debut series, AI Fundamentals, is a comprehensive guide for those seeking to understand and apply AI in various professional settings. Andrew's work caters to a broad audience, from managers to coders, breaking down AI basics, essential math, machine learning, and generative AI clearly and engagingly. His ability to demystify the complexities of AI has made him a trusted voice in the tech industry. Andrew's work imparts knowledge and empowers his readers to navigate and innovate in an AI-driven world.

$10.99 FREE EBOOK

Receive Your Free Copy of The Power of AI

SCAN ME

Or visit:
bookboundstudios.wixsite.com/andrew-hinton